Spared

www.mascotbooks.com

Spared

Cover photography by Shaun Deane
Author photograph by Al Karevy

I have tried to recreate events, locales, and conversations
from my memories of them. I may have changed some
identifying characteristics and details, such as physical
properties, occupations, places of residence, and names in
order to maintain subject anonymity. My memories are my
own, and I have recalled the stories recorded here to the
best of my ability.

For more information, please contact:
Mascot Books
620 Herndon Parkway #320
Herndon, VA 20170
info@mascotbooks.com

CPSIA Code: PRBVG0518A
Library of Congress Control Number: 2018902667
ISBN-13: 978-1-68401-754-6

Printed in the United States

Spared

a memoir

Shaun Deane

For Patricia

And for Travis and Gretchen

Finally, to Paul Cody with gratitude

Preface

Time present and time past
Are both perhaps present in time future,
And time future contained in time past.
If all time is eternally present
All time is unredeemable.
What might have been is an abstraction
Remaining a perpetual possibility
Only in a world of speculation.
What might have been and what has been
Point to one end, which is always present.
Footfalls echo in the memory
Down the passage which we did not take
Towards the door we never opened
Into the rose garden. My words echo
Thus, in your mind.

— **T. S. Eliot**
The Four Quartets
Burnt Norton

Chapter One

Buck and Me

No.

Shortly after I learned that my parents intended to divorce, in 1967, I found myself standing in front of our bathroom mirror with a large Buck knife in my right hand. "My family is imploding and I am very sad." I did not have these words.

The first swipe across my upper cheek was cursory. By applying more pressure with each stroke, eventually I had raised a welt the size of a quarter that enabled me to brag that the old man had slugged me in a drunken rage—now that we were divorced and all.

When I taught at an elite private school in Connecticut after my own divorce, forty years later, more than half the students in my classes came from fractured families; but in the spring of my fourteenth year, I was the only person I knew whose family would no longer be intact.

While I may have been stumbling, I understood the danger inherent in my family. Instincts for self-preservation turned me outward—to friends and street life.

Now, gazing through the telescope barrel from the fat end, four decades down Route 66, I have been astonished to discover how much I never knew. At the same time, there are vignettes, and especially sentences uttered, that I have carried along with me, year after year. They come in moments of insomnia or while driving alone. Sometimes, I laugh out loud, and often I have had to shake off the tears before entering the grocery store or my own kitchen at the end of the day.

I trust my memory. It has protected me from my greatest foe: ambiguity. You don't want to play me in Trivial Pursuit. I used to memorize—no, more like photocopy the license plates of friend's cars, mentally, so that I could look down at the bumper of an approaching vehicle to confirm surely, that "here comes Jim, or Peter." My best friend's phone number from 1961? That's easy.

No clarity: that's unacceptable. I once had a girlfriend who might have been described as "ethereal." Statuesque, a stunning Swede. A few months after we met, she gazed off to the distance one evening in October and murmured, "Hmmmmm."

"What?" I asked her.

"Hot snow..." she said, as if she had just had a taste of the most delicious éclair ever.

"Can't you picture it?" she said with excitement as she locked eyes with me.

"Yeah, water," I offered. I was flummoxed and not trying to be cruel. In order to survive, I felt that it was necessary to beat back any hint of ambiguity so that all things could be compartmentalized. "This is this," said Michael to Stanley in *The Deer Hunter*.

Everything here, then, is accurate. Everything is precisely as it occurred, except for the instances where it isn't.

As I rinsed the Buck knife off in the bathroom sink, I reached for a saffron colored hand towel that hung on a brass hook, shaped like a king's crown. Slowly and carefully, I dried the svelte silver blade and slid it back into its leather case with the short wraparound strap and then pushed the clasp shut with my thumb.

There was a wall mirror behind me so that I could see the back of my head reflected in the medicine chest door just in front of me. "Hair's getting long," I said aloud, but quietly.

I took a final look at my cheek, where the knuckles had hit hard, turned my jaw to the left, then the right, and snapped off the light.

Chapter Two

Same Again

The first time that I traveled overseas, I spent three weeks in Southern Ireland. I started the trip in early May and returned to New England just before Memorial Day. As I rode through my hometown in the back seat of a questionable yellow cab, I was amazed at how the large oak trees along Cabot Field had a complete set of full and open leaves where there had been only buds when I left.

It was, perhaps, one of the first times that I had truly noticed anything outside the blinders of my recently concluded adolescence. But my story begins and continues in April, "the cruelest month," where one is often teased by the promises that are realized or revoked in May.

It had been less than two weeks since I was called to my father's house at the end of my longest workday. Then, it was still light out and the trees were pushing out buds, enthusiastically. It was unusual that my stepmother made the call to begin with. And, though mysterious, I shrugged it off and made the trek cross-town since the directive had been, "Your father would like to talk with you." Formal, but that was Phyllis.

Once arrived, "Whoa. I wasn't expecting that." I uttered.

"No, I don't imagine you were," said my father in commiseration after he had described the details that the detective in Florida had passed along.

It was true that the news of my mother's death was unexpected, but it was not a shock, not really. We were linked biologically, yet we never were equipped to offer anything of substance to the other. Once my mother left for Florida, I knew, intuitively, that it would end badly, but what I didn't know yet was that this report from my father was only a dry run.

And so it was done. My innocence abolished, my bar mitzvah complete. I wouldn't need that ticket anymore—the one that had just been purchased to visit my mother in Fort Lauderdale. She had moved south about the time I started college, after a long-term suitor had proposed and she fled, moving deeper into isolation because she did not want to be at the heart of another broken family, as she described it. Al, who loved her, was still married at the time.

During the years after she moved, we made awkward attempts at reconciliation to heal a long-term rift between two redheads, their heels dug in. We had an unstated agreement to at least be civil and to explore how to re-engage in a landscape full of foxholes and barely hidden mines. But then, as if to assert her inalienable right to establish the agenda, this defining bit of punctuation.

We live by seconds. We plan for tomorrow. We review over our shoulder. But memory is non-linear, and the reconsideration and reconstruction of events includes images that seem out of place or appear to be inconsequential. Why was one detail retained and entire days rejected and missing? I understand now my wife's description that, as a child, she often wondered which side of the dream she was on, and when.

Soon I was sitting in the detective's office in Fort Lauderdale reading the note my mother had left—to me, only—with my brother Chris and father in tow. And from that afternoon, I can recall only a few sentences from the four-page letter. *"Now don't fret dear."* The few days spent in Florida united the three of us for a while. We hadn't spent any time together outside of the weekly visits to my father's house for Sunday dinner since the divorce, and this time together hearkened back to pre-divorce Friday nights, old time radio shows like The Shadow and The Green Hornet and my dad making his one and only dish, hot dogs with macaroni and cheese. Mom was never there then, either.

Then we were on the flight home and sharing a rite of passage, sealed with a beer. Male bonding, I thought, would be better around a campfire, but my dad never did take us anywhere and we were not calling the shots on this trip.

It felt good to have the funeral behind us and to be back to work after the weekend and studying again, for my final exams. My dog, a collie, was excited that our ritual was intact. She knew that a walk was in store and that the pacing, the route, and the praise would all be perfect. After all, the pack leader was back in town. "How about the junior high loop, old girl?" Her ears signaled affirmation as she slid into down dog and I slipped on a light windbreaker, grabbed the leash from the back of the doorknob to my room, and bent from the waist to stretch hamstrings constrained for too long during these past two weeks.

Heading for the door, the phone rang. It was Dad.

"Have you heard anything from Chris?" he asked.

"No. How come?"

"Well, I got a call from his work today, he didn't make it in. What do you suppose that's all about?"

Down through the years, that simple inquiry has been played over and again in the Victrola of my memory.

"He's probably processing, Dad. He's out walking or something. None of us has had any time to think about events. I'm sure he's fine." Normally, I would have seen Chris during the weekend. All through that spring he had been coming to visit on Saturday nights at the apartment I shared with other students and townies in my final semester at Brandeis. A starving student, I rarely went out on weekend nights, and with my brother buying, it was enjoyable to spend a few hours considering the upcoming baseball season. At some point, he'd introduce family topics and I would change the subject as quickly as possible. It was annoying that he wanted to explore family dynamics, not Luis Tiant, and that was at odds with my coping mechanisms, so we were each unsatisfied. My inability to finesse this area haunts me.

Washington Street bisects Newton and had to be crossed to get to the junior high school where I could remove the leash and walk the perimeter, strolling the parapets to decompress a bit before dinner.

Oddly, there was almost no traffic that evening, and the two of us got across with ease. Dusk was coming on and urged us along to the opposite end of the football field more quickly than we may have liked and eventually, back out to confront the Washington Street crossing once again. To get back to the apartment, we took two back streets through the suburban landscape. The first was just a block long, and then the short promenade to home.

We made the turn on to Gilbert Street. Maybe Sergeant Ellis would be watering his lawn. He had been a Newton police detective for years and we would exchange pleasantries and curse the Yankees.

Looking for the Sergeant, I saw a lanky figure approaching us. My roommate Jim shuffled tentatively along a hedgerow from the opposite end of the street. Such a small slice of life on a Monday evening, in April, when the world inverted. In an instant, every sensory circuit opened and was recording.

He was hesitating as he approached me and that got my attention. There was no reason for him to be out, on that street, at that moment. Involuntarily, my left hand rose to chest height, like a crossing guard providing the most basic directive.

Stop.

Heat waves rose from a tarmac that was only just barely beyond the last snowfall. The center cannot hold. Like two gunslingers from a spaghetti western, unwavering, we stood. And, like the final scene in the cemetery, from *The Good, The Bad and The Ugly*, we waited for someone to flinch. We stood, immobilized, in the gloaming. It was hushed, but there was a ringing in my ears. Slowly, like tin men, we started moving, now within one hundred yards of each other. Then, fifty. Again, we stopped.

"Shaun..."

"Stay over there, Jim."

"Doc..."

"Don't come near me." I already knew everything.

"Phyllis just called you."

"I know. Stay over there."

No recollection of getting from the street to my room. Only a block and a half, but where have those moments gone? The phone was in my hand. Jim stood awkwardly to my left, trapped within the confines of a smaller and smaller room.

"Phyllis?"

"Hello, Shaun. Your father would like you to come over. Now." The pleasure of your company is requested. RSVP, etc.

Again. Oh God. This is really happening—to me.

"Why?"

"He needs you to come over."

"I heard you. Why?"

"It's...it's bad."

"What is?"

"...bad."

Silence.

"What is?"

"It's about...Chris."

"He's dead."

"Yes, yes."

"How?"

"The same way."

The room lurched and spun. I was in a vortex, swirling, careening and bouncing off the sides of a funnel. A chasm opened beneath me. My legs were kicking at the opening, but, remarkably, I was still upright, and still with phone in hand. Recently, I awoke in this nightmare, panting, with tears streaming down my face, at 3 A.M. Deep inside the funnel, my mother's hands had been trying to grab my ankles.

"I can't come, Phyllis. I can't."

"Your father needs you."

"I can't do this again."

But I knew I would go. It was out of my hands.

After I hung up the phone, I grabbed the door to my room and slammed it as hard as I possibly could.

"Don't lose it now, Shaun," Jim said. Another haunting statement. I always thought that was a strange thing to say, as if I should save my emotions for a more appropriate time. Although I was not fully engaged in that moment, something subtle caught my attention, and in retrospect, I believe that is when my interactions with Jim became just the slightest bit guarded. Self-protection must be some sort of emotional antibody. Some level of awareness was rushing to the scene of the crime, though it has taken many long walks in the woods to see any of it.

In a sea of disbelief, I was the ship's figurehead, on the bow, experiencing the spray first hand and looking back over my shoulder to the observation deck, where all were gathered. Unable to answer their urgent, questioning faces, I could only respond with a shrug of perplexed confusion—these were uncharted waters.

Chapter Three

Betty

It was time to make the yearly pilgrimage to "The Shoe Barn," on Kempton Place in West Newton, with Betty, my mother. We usually went just before Labor Day, in preparation for the new school year. The Barn was located in a valley below Washington Street and was adjacent to the taxi company I would work at some years down the road. One entered the building through two green swinging doors, each of which included a large pane of reinforced glass embedded with wire in a diamond pattern and a long rubber sweep on the bottom of each side. Once inside the main foyer, it was the smells that I remember most. In the anteroom, it was a rich brew of Jack Purcell and Converse rubber; through another set of swinging doors and it was a full-on assault of brown shoe leather.

During this visit, I lobbied relentlessly for a very specific version of black boots with Cuban heels. It was 1965, and the Beatles had been sitting atop the record charts for more than a year and I was about to enter middle school. I needed to establish an image and there was no solitary piece of gear that could make that happen better than a pair of satin-finished, over the ankle Chelsea boots, just like John's, or Paul's.

Betty was unconvinced. My desire to make a statement was at odds with what she described as the need for practicality. This offset, ultimately, would become a part of the battlefield we would traverse over the next decade and a half. What I have come to appreciate is that "practicality" really was not the issue. Her unstated objection arose from the myriad ways she had worked to remain unnoticeable throughout her life, as she labored to divert attention from the disfigurement her polio had created.

That polio, from 1931, had left her right leg an inch and a half shorter than her left, and a full shoe size smaller as well. My enthusiasm for the striking black boots with a zipper up the instep and the seriously pointed toes may have been in competition with the tedium Mom must have felt when, just as in previous years, she had to ask for two pairs of the same shoe—"one in a four and a half and one in a five and a half."

I wonder how many times it was that I heard that exact phrase uttered and in how many shoe stores across the Greater Boston area. Somewhere, at various Goodwill or Salvation Army stores, there was a team of mismatched shoes: artifacts of our annual trek, each with a five and a half for the right foot and a four and a half for the left foot. What were the odds of a customer for those?

Elizabeth Anne Riley was born just two years before the stock market crash and the start of the Great Depression. When the polio struck a few years later, it just seemed like one more dose from the tainted well, according to her father Frank. He and my grandmother, Alice, were able to scrape together enough money to fit Betty with a brace and an elevated shoe, but she did not want an appendage that screamed "look at me" and preferred to take her chances and let the pronounced limp speak for itself. She explained that the brace was simply uncomfortable and never wore it again.

The pattern, established then—so early—was repeated throughout her life: with suitors, children, employers, and any challenge that was remotely frustrating. Suck it up and move on. As a strategy, it was effective for self-preservation, but the "stiff upper lip" approach ultimately *was* the handicap, and it affected every relationship she had, or could have had. "I don't know why she was that way," her sister Pat explained, "and we just let her be. I don't think we had any idea about how to deal with it, and she rejected any offer of assistance out of hand. After she got married, it seemed clear that she wanted distance from the family." And when she scrawled that final sentence, it was a summation that tied a lifetime of emotional denial up succinctly using just four words.

How do we resolve the boxes of inherited photographs and small format movies with stories and anecdotes from the tribe, not to mention our own riddled memory of the day-to-day events from a hazy pre-adolescent fog bank?

The shutter snares an inflected eyebrow, or a side glance—a gaze of longing toward a distant, unseen horizon, captured in 1/500th of a second, on an overcast afternoon, and stamped SEPT 1963, but the sinew that connects to the family backstory cannot be deciphered.

Betty at the animal farm with a green silk scarf surrounding her stunning, auburn hair—her inheritance from Enniskillen—holding an ice cream cone full of peanuts above her head and away from the llama just behind her left shoulder. She looks joyous and invigorated. She is fully present. She is authentic.

In another image, the couple—Paul and Betty at a backyard summer family gathering. The photo screams "1962." Dad faces the camera directly and has his fingers interlocked around her 23-inch waist. He grins maniacally and looks like a scientist from the Manhattan Project and not unlike the father from "Back to the Future." He seeks the limelight.

She is leaning into him (or is that simply the way her weaker leg has caused her to support herself on the uneven backyard grass at Aunt Pat's house?) and wears a stylish size six jumper with a slight silver sheen and her shoulder length hair offers a nod to Jackie, in the sweep, up and back from her forehead. She looks off to her right with a forced grin and has her arms intertwined behind her own back. No reciprocity of touch. A subtle look of "What am I doing here?" on her face.

I could not appreciate the signs of disconnection that surrounded us (their single beds, the absence of "family time," the strident chill of dinners that had no inherent love in the preparation). In fact, my only memory of marital turbulence during this time was of my father struggling with a frozen front door, cursing, and my mother's sarcasm from the second floor: "Temper, temper, little man." My father was five feet and seven inches tall.

Shortly after those photos were added to the family album, Betty started working weekends at the Boston Lying-In Hospital cafeteria on shifts that kept her away from home from Friday afternoon until Sunday evening.

When the going gets tough, the tough get going.

Betty's self-imposed exile every weekend created a platform whereby my father became, inevitably, the good cop. The fun began on Friday evenings with old time radio rebroadcasts of *The Shadow*, *Suspense*, and *The Green Hornet*.

"Who knows what evil lurks in the hearts of men?"

"Tired of the ordinary? Want to get away from it all? We offer you...SUSPENSE!" And then that blood chilling organ line.

Simple food, fun food, was his specialty: hot dogs, macaroni and cheese, and sometimes breakfast for dinner. On Saturday afternoons, he would take us and a few other neighborhood kids to the Paramount Theatre for a triple-header: a cartoon, an episode of an ongoing serial with a cliffhanger at the end of every episode, and then the main feature. We'd walk the three-mile round trip along Washington Street, under the canopy of centuries old oak trees and past the Jackson Homestead, which had been a stop on the Underground Railway during the mid 1800s.

In between these activities, my father worked on his thesis, sometimes sitting cross-legged in the living room and surrounded by stacks of 3x5 inch index cards. On Sunday night, there was the changing of the guards, but the first time we saw Betty again was, typically, on Monday morning before school.

One evening in the middle of the week—a Tuesday, I believe—my mother came to the room I shared with my brother and blurted, "Your father is leaving. Oh, God. I don't want him to go." Then, her tears as she pulled me into a foreign country—within her arms.

No foreshadowing. No screaming matches, no plates hurled against the kitchen wall. No intercepted phone calls from lovers. Like every emotional milestone, once again, we had been blind-sided. The slog toward acceptance was easy compared to the confusion of an intimate encounter with my mother.

My chin, on her shoulder, bounced lightly with each of her convulsive sobs as I confronted my brother's gaze from the other twin bed. He was flushed and on the verge of nervous church laughter, given half a chance. Neither of us understood that this was the beginning of the unraveling.

Then, like prizefighters who enjoy a respite every three minutes, we were back to neutral corners and the familiarity of isolation and silence.

At 40 Walker Street in 1967, the tectonic plates of a union crafted in post-World War II optimism had settled and could not support the ongoing needs of my father—a narcissistic, only child whose mother's interest in Christian Science meant that medical as well as emotional support was withheld, and Frank Riley's third daughter, damaged by polio at three, who had determined early on that the unflinching British way would get one through.

Such irony, that the weekend crew was reunited fifteen years later on an Eastern Airlines flight to Florida to repatriate Mom. We landed before noon and went directly to see the detective that had called my father two days earlier.

Three metal chairs with a very thin layer of brown vinyl padding sat in front of Detective Arden's desk in the Fort Lauderdale police station. The chairs were arranged in a triangle with one directly in front and two behind. I took the lead position. Without any discussion, I had been promoted to first chair in this hastily formed orchestra.

Jim Arden had a thin comb over that complemented a nicely tanned pate. He wore gold-rimmed aviator glasses and held a new and recently sharpened No. 2 Dixon Ticonderoga pencil in his left hand that he was moving idly in a small circular motion. Once we were settled in, he broke the ice.

"Our whole office is very sorry for your loss," Arden started.

A long pause, during which it became clear that his comments were directed to me. Isn't the dad supposed to drive?

"Thanks," I managed.

"We were called on Monday morning because your mother had not arrived to work at the bank. Two officers were dispatched to the house and couldn't get a response at the door."

No response—that's a 10-7, I thought, *or perhaps a 10-30*.

"Officer Gale circled the house and was able to observe that there was someone in the car, in the garage. It was then that we called a locksmith so that we could open the doors."

Nope, definitely a 10-56.

He mentioned something about my mother's manager at the bank and that the gas to the house had been shut off, but I was only absorbing about half of what was being ramrodded my way.

He reached across the desk and handed me a small light yellow envelope with some transparent spring flowers on one of the upper corners. The envelope had been opened and I could see that it was addressed to me with my complete address in Newton but was not stamped. *That's odd*, I thought. *Why the address, if it was going to be in the car with her?*

At every job I have ever had there were yearly performance assessments. In the best companies, these were checklist events, no surprises. If the environment was healthy, the feedback offered was a summary—a simple recap of what was already known.

In less healthy companies, and especially with less astute

managers, the feedback was withheld until review day, forcing an awkward, silent reading session during which the employee had to try and absorb a lot of critical and complementary information in real time. I usually found myself thinking afterwards about the things I wished I had said or at least expressed better.

And so there I sat, in an unanticipated performance review, watching an enormous black fly land repeatedly on the desk before me, as Detective Arden waved at it and looked back at me implacably.

The letter had four pages, folded in half, numbered (and circled) at the top of each page. I carried this letter from house to house for almost thirty years. After my divorce was assured and I was clearing out my belongings from the home in Rhode Island, I threw the letter away.

A fresh start! No baggage. Now, I wish I could reference it directly, but a few sentences still exist in the back eddies of my memory.

"Dear Shaun—I address this to you, though of course it is for Christopher too."

It was already starting on an offbeat, I thought.

Later down the page: *"Now don't fret dear...I just can't continue to go on in a world so full of pain."*

At the bottom of the second page: *"I left Mini and Maxi out in the backyard with plenty of food. I suppose you'll need to get them to an animal shelter."*

Then, in conclusion: *"It might seem a cruel final note, but Fuck the Whole World."*

I noticed the capitals, and when I turned back to page one, I saw a stain in the upper right corner of the page. A tear? Coffee? It was not lost on me that this was aggression and it made me uncomfortable that my brother had been excluded. As if inclusion was an honor.

I was tired. Profoundly exhausted. I bowed my head and though I did not want to, not there, not then; some tears. A hand patted my shoulder from behind. Dad.

I reached around to my right without looking and handed the letter off to Chris. "Here you go, bro'."

When I looked back up, the fly was just landing on the black handset of the desk telephone.

None of us wanted to stay in Florida any longer than we had to, but the requirements for cremation meant that there was a cooling off period—literally—before the ashes could be moved.

Back at Mom's house, I felt like an intruder. No chair was comfortable. We made a run to the local Kroger's for the standard weekend menu from years before, but that night there was no Shadow or Green Hornet. Beer had some appeal, though the selection was only average. We did what we had to do.

The cats were in the backyard and we still had to deal with them before we left the state. At one point, in search of their food, I opened the door to the garage, gagged and recoiled from the overwhelming smell of car exhaust. I slammed the door shut, and hard. Ever since, in traffic or perhaps walking past a car warming up on a winter morning, that smell transports me back to May, and Fort Lauderdale.

On the sideboard, next to a small wooden dining table, sat Mom's mini-bar. Front and center, a half-gallon bottle of Gilbey's gin, which had been her go-to drink for as long as I could remember. The bottle was rough to the touch, like fine grade sandpaper, and as a kid, I'd wet my finger and run it down the side of the bottle, briefly revealing the level line inside as it faded back to an ambiguous frost.

In high school, I would sometimes pilfer some of the gin, replacing what had been purloined with water. I could usually get away with two or three thefts, safely. During those times, I imagine that Mom's intake went up. I read once that gin has over three hundred ingredients and, as a result, everyone is allergic to something in the liquor, contributing to a hangover or big behavior (or both). Once, on a trip to Nantucket, from the bar car on the train to the cross-sound boat, I watched Charlie consume 34 gin and tonics before we had even docked the ferry.

Nothing to read, nowhere to hide, not much to say, so shortly after dark, I pulled the cushions off the couch, flipped them over, and made up a crude bed on the floor. At every turn, I was doing whatever I could to disassociate from my surroundings.

Dad took the master bedroom, sleeping in a dead ex-wife's bed.

On Thursday, we took the two refugees, Mini and Maxi, to the Broward County Humane Society. It was unfair and I apologized to them. I told them shit happens. Then, a pre-GPS cross-town drive to the Larkin Crematorium to pick up Mom. The urn they gave us looked like a cocktail shaker from Casablanca, and I was shocked by how much it weighed.

Later that afternoon I sat in seat 18D with a blue plastic Swiss Air carry-on bag at my feet, lugging Mom back to New England. Christopher sat directly behind me in 19D, and my father was across the aisle in 18C. We each ordered a Budweiser shortly after takeoff.

The snacks that were provided included a small round and stale bulkie roll of some sort. Chris said, "These things are like buffalo chips," bringing a smile from the rest of the team. It was a three-hour flight, so we opted for a second Bud, and as the flight attendant was starting to walk back up the aisle, Chris, not using his quiet voice said, "Oh and another one of those buffalo chips, please!"

It was dumb, but it was funny. All of us laughing hard for the first time in days and, for a change of pace, tears of laughter. *My brother can be pretty funny,* I thought—a bit of a surprise.

One week later, he'd be gone too.

November 22, 1976

Dear Chris,

I have opened two savings accounts. One is a joint account with you, the other a joint with Shaun. I will need your signature on this card, directly under mine (write, do not print). If you will then put it in an envelope and mail it, no postage necessary, I would appreciate it.

This has nothing to do with your taxes (you don't have to declare any interest). In case I kick the bucket, this just will make it easier for you and Shaun to collect. After I have been with the bank for three months, I will also have life insurance. Again, you and Shaun are the beneficiaries. The bank pays for this, but I forgot to ask how much. They also gave me medical coverage after three months. I will write again and send name of bank, address and phone number. Hope all is well with you.

Love,

Mom

Chapter Four

Couldn't Take It

After two funerals in as many weeks, one might expect some sort of finality, but, as I discovered, the fun was just beginning. There was no User Guide for the situation I found myself in and I was barely able to interpret the signals that I was receiving. Everything was so overwhelming that I seemed to have lost the ability to discriminate between intuition, what I thought I had heard, what was unfolding before me, and what was the actual reality of the situation. My expectations of people's behavior, and, sometimes, their motives was upended, frequently.

Stories that juxtaposed illusion and reality had always fascinated me. Now, I was in a lead role. When things got heated in my first marriage, my wife would sometimes exclaim that I was not dealing with reality.

My canned response, intended for a laugh (at least from me), was that "reality is overrated." Yet, knowing what is real, what is true and valid, has become my Excalibur. I am empowered with my hands on the hilt and at sea when it slips from my grip.

Once I learned that Christopher had died, that was it for work as far as I was concerned. I never called in, I never quit, and I never cared. I don't know what I was thinking about for income, other than the fact that I was now executor of two estates and that ought to be good for the odd meal out. I was able to come and go as I needed to, and, at least to begin with, I could avoid situations that I knew would be a challenge. Essentially, that was every human encounter. Since I was in my final semester in college, I shared an apartment with five others. A few days after the second funeral, I returned to the apartment for the first time around mid-morning.

The two-story house was one of the older ones in the neighborhood on a connector street between Routes 16 and 30—parts of the Boston Marathon route. We lived on the second floor. Normally, I'd have parked my car in back and entered through the rear of the house, but that day I parked out front in the pullout and took the front steps two at a time. Then, in the front door and up the carpeted stairs to the second-floor landing, just outside my bedroom, which was the first room to the right. The top of the stairs was part of a public area that included a short hallway to the kitchen, a table for the common house phone, and, on the right, the only bathroom.

As I got to the landing, one of my roommates came out of his room, which was directly across the hall from mine. I was not expecting to see Ron, or anyone really, as everyone was either a student or employed, so the house was typically vacant for the majority of the daylight hours. Ron was one of the longer-term tenants and somewhat outside the mainstream demographic in that he was neither a student, a cab driver, or a musician. He worked as a draftsman or a PC board assembler and pumped all of his earnings into his toys. He had an immaculate 1967 Buick Skylark, which was not a particularly sexy car, but it was flawless and so too was his R100 BMW with the Vetter fairing. For those of us limping along on Hamburger Helper and older VW bugs that were a week-to-week proposition, the sheer efficiency of his operation was a marvel and created some envy—particularly on those cold mornings when I had to pick up the first kids for the high school bus run and my car was unresponsive and without heat. He had an annoying habit of rubbing it in a bit when things went south, and in my pre-funeral mentality, I may have noticed this, but not consciously. That was about to change a lot.

"Hey," said Ron.

"Hey yourself."

"Where have you been?" he challenged. Warning. Danger Will Robinson. This was the first of what would become thousands of such encounters. One part of my radar system knew fundamentally that he must have had some inkling of recent events for Mr. Yours Truly, and Oh Man Are You Really Going To Make Me Say It?

I had not even considered an encounter like this yet, and as a result, I was making it up on the fly.

"Well, ah, ah, my brother. Well, he died."

"Oh yeah, I think I heard about that."

See? See? You think? I don't think; I know. But I'm feeling so fucking addled at the moment that all I can do is push some more of that adrenaline into my already tumbling stomach cavity.

"What happened?"

Really? This is happening? I have to do this? That is, how do I do this? What am I doing here? I feel hot. My knees are shaky.

"He…That is, he…"

Ron wasn't going to take no for an answer, I could see that. In fact, he had leaned in even closer. You know, because he knew, yet had to hear it with his own hairy ears—from the source.

"Well, he killed himself."

And without missing a beat, and to my profound amazement, he replied, "Huh! Couldn't take it." Not a question, a declaration. His smug summary, his assessment, his need to put something in a box so that he would not have to confront the irrationality of it all.

I could never possibly suggest what I might have expected his response to be, but this was so far off the charts that I was unable to come up with anything at all, though every fiber in my body felt that roundhouse right coming from below my waist, past my shoulder, and squarely into those round gold glasses frames—hard. With enthusiasm. Then, like that iconic photo of Muhammad Ali standing over Sonny Liston, prostrate on the mat in Lewiston, Maine: me, daring him to get back up.

Instead, I pivoted on my heel and slithered in to my room, shut the door, heaved convulsively, and fell to my knees. Tears like a garden hose, no end in sight. And for years, no, decades, I replayed that scene over and over and over again wondering why, why, why had I not thrown that right? At that time though, at that moment, I was only at the cusp of my anger and any understanding at all. A Buddhist will tell you that that's attachment and that attachment creates suffering. It was, and it did.

* * *

Even long-established relationships were changing. Jim and I were inseparable best friends in high school. The two of us, along with five other sixteen or seventeen year old boys, traveled cross-country in two Volkswagen buses in 1970. The first time I heard "Ohio" was that summer when I pushed a quarter into the jukebox in Joplin, Missouri, and the clientele started murmuring about "longhairs."

I had been keeping a low profile for a while. My activities were focused on the lower segments of the Maslow hierarchy of needs (Physiological and Safety) with only vague hopes for Love, let alone Self-Esteem and the real long shot: Self-Actualization. Food, sleep, shelter, and basic comfort were about as far out as my limited vision even wanted to see.

Still, I had some suspicions that I was being observed. I still lived in Newton, the small city I grew up in and, as a result, I was pretty well connected, socially. I had an uncanny sense that people were watching me whenever I was out in public. I could see something in their eyes, a very slight cock of the head, a searching, questioning sort of posture. "Well, you're not headed down that path too, are you?" is what I imagined they were thinking. It felt like every public outing was a stage performance at a time when I most wanted the limelight pointed in the opposite direction.

The compulsion to "be OK" was so strong that I spent little time determining how to get to that place. In hindsight, it's easy to see the models that I was working from—especially the ways in which my mom had put her hands on the plow and just held on, moving forward, along the field rows.

As my college days wound down, and before Chris died, my plans were ill formed. I believed that things would work out and that opportunities would present themselves and that my university enlightenment and incremental maturity would make what was unknown obvious.

But then that high, inside fastball brushed me back from the plate, and from that point on, the way in which I presented myself became a much bigger priority than how I actually was. The ensuing decades were like one extended out of body experience as I reached for straws of normalcy, while in a very deep place what I needed most was to return to the start, with, as Buddhism suggests, "beginner eyes." When I finally understood that belief systems are simply models that have been provided to us (by our parents, mostly) and that they can be swapped for something more relevant, it was truly a "Hallelujah" moment after a four-decade search for the return ticket to that platform I'd been standing on when the family began to unravel.

The extent to which the ground was unstable in general, and particularly in the metamorphosis of my long-term relationship with Jim, was made clear just a few weeks later.

By now, it was late May, and Bob, another close friend, was urging a night out. It was one of the first nights when a tee shirt would suffice and we had determined that a trip to the El Phoenix Room on the Boston line was in order. The facility was an odd combination of an Irish workingman's bar and a Mexican restaurant, and it was where most of us had been served our first underage beer with no concern about getting our licenses checked.

We met at the apartment in West Newton and piled into my car, outside the front door. Bob was riding shotgun and Jim was in the back seat with a co-worker from Piroli's Construction yard. I had not met Kevin before this. He was from Watertown and we did not travel in the same circles. As I fished my keys out of my left-hand pocket, I looked out at the etherized sky with just two potato puff clouds over the Mobil station at the end of the street. It felt good to be breaking out of my cloistered routine, and I was glad we were doing something simple. No hiccups in sight. I had just inserted my key in the ignition slot and was about to start the engine when from directly behind me, Kevin started talking at a volume level that was just a notch higher than necessary and that made me jump a bit.

"Oh man. Did you guys hear about that kid over here in Newton?"

Uh oh.

Stomach acid was being released again. I looked down at the ribbed grey floor mat. Where was this headed? No one had taken the bait, though someone must have said something— even "No"—to urge him forward.

"Well, first his mother killed herself and then, like...I don't know a week later, his brother did the same thing in the same way! I mean wow! How fucked up is that?"

I felt dizzy. My face was hot. And it seemed to me that there was some sort of reverb in the car. An echo hung in the air. It's not at all clear what my expectation was about where the discourse was headed next. Without missing a beat though, I heard Jim start to speak and as I glanced up at the rearview mirror, I think I caught a bit of a smile.

"Well, yep. That's him right there," he said, as he pointed to me.

I was stunned and absolutely speechless. The space inside the microbus had compressed and I felt claustrophobic. Again (and again and again) I had to question what I had just experienced— did that just happen?

I looked back into the rearview mirror and my eyes connected once more with Jim's. Any number of resources will tell you that

70% of communication is non-verbal or that "the eyes are the window to the soul." I'm certain that my gaze was beseeching: What are you doing, Jim? For the moment that our eyes met, all I can recall is a complete lack of response.

Now, I turned to my right and locked eyes with Bob, who (in support?) had been gazing at the floor, too.

"Do you believe this shit?" I asked. To his credit, and while some backpedaling was happening behind me, he just shook his head. In one instant, Bob's head shake solidified a close relationship we had until he died of cancer thirty years later, and Jim's utter lack of protection for me drove us apart. Once again it seemed that my existence was being manipulated by the smallest intervals of time and pluck.

Chapter Five

Cum Laude

Just a few days later, with the sun streaming into my room and warming up the southeast corner of my bed, I was sifting through a large pile of documents from the realtor who was handling the sale of my mother's house in Fort Lauderdale and the monument company that was doing the artwork for Christopher's gravestone.

I was alone in the house and made it to the phone by the third ring.

"Hello, may I speak to Shaun, please?"

"This is Shaun speaking."

"Shaun, it's Dean Palmer, at Brandeis, how are you?"

"I'm alright, how about you?"

"Fine, fine," she replied.

It was Tuesday and just after lunch, though I wasn't eating so well since Christopher's burial.

About six months before this, one of my housemates had replaced the coiled wire that ran to the handset with an extra-long version from Radio Shack so that it was possible to pull the phone into any of the three bedrooms that surrounded the small hallway and to close the door for a modicum of privacy. The three tenants on the third floor were forced to have a more public airing of their issues and had to accept the privileges of longer-term residents. Everyone had to defer to a trip wire across the main thoroughfare during prime time.

So far, I could not imagine what this call was all about. Perhaps it had something to do with my robe or cap. When I was in high school, they had to custom order a mortar board for me because my large red afro forced my hat size way to the right—an "8," which one simply never sees when ordering hats. "Big squash," I thought to myself and a slight smile (the first in a few days) curled the edges of my mouth.

"I've been reviewing your transcript and it appears as though you did not take your final exam in Modern Art (an elective)."

"That's true," I said. I still saw nothing on the horizon.

"Well, Shaun (when someone starts using my name every few paragraphs, my radar starts spinning), "that's a real problem for graduation day, then."

"So who would like to begin today?"

MacMurphy raised his hand.

"I've been thinking about what you said about getting things off your chest, and today, as you may or may not know, is the opening of the World Series. And I'd like to suggest that we change the work detail to tonight so that we can watch the ball game."

"Well, Mr. MacMurphy, what you're asking is that we change a very carefully worked out schedule and some men on the ward take a long time to get used to the schedule."

Then came the vote, and the smug sneer of satisfaction on Nurse Ratched's lips as policy overwhelmed circumstance.

I had never met with or spoken to Dean Palmer before, but I had an uncanny visual image of Louise Fletcher as we talked that afternoon.

"Whoa, whoa, whoa..." I said. "Graduation is in ten days. I'm all done."

"Well, that can't work, Shaun, as all of your requirements have not been fulfilled."

Now, my Irish was up. I could feel the familiar flush running north from the holding tank in my gut to that oversized squash. For the past two or three weeks, I had been in a deep fog, it seemed. It had been impossible to aim at anything, to direct my confusion or anger at anything at all. There was nothing tangible to point at. My pulse was climbing and I could feel the increased thump in my chest.

The mist was parting a bit and every self-protective molecule in my being was on standby.

"I think, if you review my transcript further, you will see a steady and consistent record of improvement. In fact, I'm running a solid 4.0 in all courses this semester and, I might add, I've worked 30 hours a week on top of all this."

I was out of breath. This was the longest set of words I had uttered in three weeks.

"Well, that is not actually true, as the final exam we are discussing wasn't taken."

"My instructor approved that! "

"Calm down now, Shaun."

Nurse Ratched, Nurse Ratched, Nurse Ratched.

Neutral corners, count of ten.

"So as you can see, we have a real problem on our hands."

I could feel this slipping away and—Lord give me strength—were my energy stores ever depleted. I really did not want to get into the details, but this wall of resistance demanded it. Take a breath.

"Dean Palmer, three weeks ago, my mother died in Florida. I had to figure out a way to deal with all of that and to finish up my last semester at the same time. Ten days later, my brother died. We buried him last Thursday. I finished all of my work in every course, I have satisfied all financial obligations to the university. When Professor Langford heard of my situation, and since the course was not part of my major, she said she would excuse me from the final."

"Well, I'm truly sorry for your loss, but she was not authorized to make that offer."

Ratched.

"Well, she did and I'll suggest that the rules around what can or cannot be offered is really between the administration and the faculty. How would I have known this?"

"Well, Shaun, by doing this, we would be establishing a precedent for the future."

Excepting the fact that it was redundant, I had a visceral reaction to that last statement. Beyond the utter insensitivity, the logic was completely flawed. I had an image of some World War II soldier falling on a plunger that ignited a set of explosives and my entire torso exploded. Now, I was in a full-on scream—a howl—yanking every morsel of anger and indignation about the abject unfairness of it all—not just this graduation discussion, but all of it. All the accumulated grief, regret, sadness, and the powerlessness I had ever stuffed, surfaced with that simple button push.

"Do you really—really, in your wildest sense of perverted logic—think that you'll ever have to worry about precedent for a student who has lost two family members to suicide in two weeks and was offered a break by a kind soul on your staff? Come on, Dean Palmer. Let's do the right thing here, and by the way, given my GPA, I am eligible for graduation, cum laude. How is that going to be affected?"

"Well, obviously if the final was not taken, that is going to draw down the GPA."

"FUCK!" I yelled as loud as I possibly could.

"Shaun, are you alright? Is there anyone there with you?"

Castrating bitch, now this, on top of it all.

"Yes, I'm alright! Are you alright? Because you are most definitely not doing what is fair or right."

Enough. Somehow, I'd ended up back in the hallway and I slammed the phone down. I'm surprised the cradle survived.

I stumbled across the fraying grey wall-to-wall carpet that was raised in a few places where a bathroom pipe had leaked in the previous year and knelt on my bed. I curled my knees to my chest and let the tears come. So many tears. Buckets of tears.

An hour passed—at least that. I must have drifted off. The phone was ringing again.

No.

Get up, shuffle off to Buffalo.

"Hello," I croaked.

A man this time. "Shaun?"

"Yeah?" I was still very groggy. My eyes were crusty from tears.

"Shaun, this is Larry Fuchs at Brandeis." Larry was the Chairman of the American Studies Department (my major). I had seen him around the department offices, and I suspect he recognized me as a departmental student, but I had never taken a course with him. I knew that he had been the first Peace Corps Director in the Philippines.

He didn't wait for me to say anything.

"Shaun, I've spoken with Dean Palmer and…"

I interrupted him and started to explain but he said, "No, wait," so I did.

"There's not going to be any issue with graduation. I wanted to let you know that as soon as I could."

"Oh wow, thank you, Larry."

Balloon deflates.

"I believe you are also on the list to graduate cum laude, too. Isn't that right?"

"It is, yes."

"Well, that's great. Congratulations, that's something to be proud of."

"I am, very much so," I stammered.

"I was wondering if you might be able to stop in and see me sometime later this week. Just to talk. Is that a possibility?"

"Sure, yes. That would be fine."

"How about Thursday afternoon, maybe 2 o'clock?"

"That's perfect."

And it was.

When I left Dr. Fuchs's office on Thursday afternoon at a little before 3 P.M., I stopped on the top grey flagstone step of the Heller School building and looked across the parking lot at two magnificent, fully formed trees dancing together in the late spring. One was a maple and the other a huge weeping willow.

It was the first time in over a month that I had taken a chance to look up, out, or across. I pulled in a long sweet breath of air, still moist with the morning dew. It was a huge relief to consider something other than myself, or my pain. It was one of those "Every day I wake up with this damned thing called hope" moments, all brought on by a simple act of kindness and sensitivity.

Shaun Deane, B.A. American Studies, cum laude.

It had a nice ring of completion to it, but because I was still so buried in the role of estate executor, it was a hollow victory. I paused briefly to honor the moment before crossing the campus road to my aging VW bug.

Chapter Six

Something in a Tweed

In a photo album I started shortly after his death, there is an out-of-focus eight-by-ten inch picture of Christopher on a street corner in Dublin. His hair is askew and he is wearing a heather colored tweed jacket with a newspaper folded under one arm. It was easy to see how the DNA had traveled, based on the hair alone. His: dark and wavy with a curl tucked in behind his left ear—his father's son. Mine: red, bushy curls from Mom. The picture is interesting because, typically, he would have had his grey Donegal hat perched at an angle over that hair, but on this windy day, it was au naturel. Details were important to him—in his dress, in the way his bureau top was arranged, and ultimately in the way he planned his final moments.

After he died, I went to his room to help my father pack things up. From the wall opposite the bed, a poster of Rudolph Nureyev in an impossible pose saying, "Try this." Between the windows, an elongated poster of Clint Eastwood—cheroot clenched in the side of his mouth, serape tossed over his right shoulder to expose a gleaming six-shooter—squinted his displeasure.

This was all on the third floor of a large rambling stucco house on the better side of Walnut Street, just up the hill from the high school. It was the home of Tom Martin and his wife Leigh and their five children, though three, only, remained at home. Tom Martin was a psychiatrist on Marlboro Street in Boston—a very high rent location—and Leigh was a social worker in the Newton

School system. Her specialty was adolescents and Chris was not the first stray that had been offered refuge in their home. In his case, it was after my mother had moved to Florida, just as he was completing high school.

The house sat at the top of the street, and some of the stucco was crumbling on the corner of the facade, by the sunroom. As I tripped on the brick walkway, which had settled in a few spots, I considered what it might mean to maintain a house of this size. *"Must be like the Golden Gate Bridge,"* I thought, *"finish painting on the Sausalito side and head back over to San Francisco to start all over again."*

At the end of the walk, there were two broad steps that presented a massive front door made of an expensive hardwood that should have been oiled more often than it was. *Probably oak*, I thought. The door was open, and in early May, it was clear that we were headed into the first eighty-degree day of the young season.

Inside, a broad stairway with a walnut bannister swung off to the left and led upstairs to what had been Christopher's room until the previous week. There is a scene in The Deer Hunter where Michael is in Vietnam, trying to convince the extremely damaged Nick to return to the United States. Nick says, "I like the trees, you know? I like the way the trees are on the mountains, all different. The way the trees are."

Ascending the stairs that day, the trees and, in particular, the bulbous oak on the front lawn drove a steady breeze in through the French windows that faced Kearsarge Road. An enthusiastic chickadee demanded my attention from a branch just outside the window that almost touched the side of the house. But not a single word exchanged between father and son in that cocoon of a room on the third floor can I recall from that Thursday.

We had a few boxes, a garment bag, and one old suitcase in hand. We didn't need much, as Chris did not have much. Mostly, he was a collector of desktop items: a box of matches from the Ritz-Carlton in London, a half-yard ale glass that sat in its own wooden frame, and a set of medium weight darts with brass shafts. The glass was fluted at the top with a long narrow shaft that connected to a round bulb at the bottom.

About a year earlier, I had asked, "How much beer do you think that half-yard glass can hold?" Shortly, we learned that it held exactly two twelve-ounce bottles of beer, though ale was better and Bass was best. Taking things to the most obvious next level, the question became, "Do you think we could drink that whole thing without putting it down?"

It was, in fact, possible. The start of the procedure was straightforward. The top of the glass was like any other, in that it was somewhat broader than the shaft. As the exercise proceeded, it became much more challenging to hoist the bottom bulb, now at arm's length, while peering down the inside of the elongated tube, all the while working out some form of rotary breathing so that you could swallow without suffocating. Chris went first and the belch he let loose when he placed the glass back in the holder caused my collie, Sly, to run from the room.

When we were young, Chris had an impressive ability to swallow air and to burp at will. My friends and I would egg him on to see how many syllables he could utter while belching the air back up. Sometimes he'd rub his stomach and complain that "I can't push any more down." We'd disabuse him of that notion and offer great encouragement that yes, he could. He must! It was important! "We All Live in a Yellow Submarine" was our favorite, but this historic burp from the half yard glass was better. Much better.

Whatever we removed from his room that day ended up in the attic of my father's house, south of Boston. I considered that someday, when my father passed on, I'd be reversing the exercise, when I would purge his belongings and get reacquainted with Christopher's one final time.

The oak tree shook itself, from the branches that almost

touched the lawn, in a rush along the massive trunk to the new shoots that strained toward the sun, twenty feet higher than the roof. The tree offered some auditory ambiance and relief from the closeness in the small room on the top floor, with the blue dappled walls and the father who had not shed a tear in my presence since the night we found out.

We assigned ourselves specific tasks, silently. My father was working on the bureau and I was pulling clothes out of the closet. Without a plan, the boxes and suitcases were a jumble of unrelated items that carried with them a presumption that everything would be sorted out at a later date. No need to get everything figured out on the fly. Now, I was down to a few remaining items only, mostly outerwear, including the tweed jacket from that Dublin photograph. I had always wanted a classic tweed jacket, but the difference in our frames precluded any notion of a "hand-me-down" to honor Chris, so I placed it carefully inside a gray garment bag from Macy's, laid out on the now stripped bed.

"Did you get this jacket for Chris, Dad?"

His arms were in a square cardboard box, up to his elbows, and he stopped for a moment and looked at me vacantly for five seconds that felt like a few minutes.

"The what?" He seemed irritated.

"This jacket. He wore it all the time. I was just wondering where it came from."

"I think...Well, I don't really..." He drifted off.

"It's OK, Dad. Doesn't matter. I was just curious."

He shook his head and looked back into the box in front of him.

It would be many months until I reconnected with that jacket.

Chapter Seven

Crazy for the Boys

The funeral for Chris took place on my birthday. After it was over, I returned to the Martin's house, carrying an ice-cold case of Heineken. Most of Chris's friends had gathered there, and some of mine as well.

Charlie was there. I first met Charlie in my sophomore year in high school, shortly after I watched him perform the death scene from "Becket," with Ted Reidy playing the non-speaking part of Thomas à Becket, prostrate on the ping pong table at Newman House, an after school "safe house" of sorts where it was alright to smoke cigarettes and offered sanctuary from the biting winds of early February.

Charlie had the biggest personality I had ever encountered. He was more well-read than anyone I knew, including most of my English teachers. He was a natural on the stage (for the senior year production of *Guys and Dolls*, he memorized every part, providing invaluable assistance in the form of a hushed whisper to many first-time thespians) and a riveting storyteller, which is where his strengths truly shone.

Later, fueled by Heineken on this early May afternoon, he was impersonating Bob Dylan, singing "Lily, Rosemary and the Jack of Hearts". After finishing the sixteenth verse (verbatim), he scanned the faces of everyone close by, leaned forward with his palms cupped over his knees and roared, "What an *insane* genius!" He was such a welcome distraction during the most unexplainable week of my life, and I loved him for it.

In addition to the large house up above the high school, the Martins owned a second home in Southeastern Massachusetts. After Chris died, and since I had stopped working entirely, it was easy to accept the invitation to join the crew—Chris's crew—at that bayside house for a weekend in late May, and where I would find myself on many occasions during the next year or two. No forward plan yet; just trying for the basics—sleep and sustenance.

Suicide is cruel. It leaves the survivors with the inevitable, single-word question: *Why?* I had been leading a life quite apart from my family members for many years, even though I was only in my early twenties. Now, I was forced to backtrack, searching for breadcrumbs.

Although I knew that most of my family was deeply depressed, self-protection was at the top of my survival pyramid, so I maintained that focus and did not get distracted by other considerations.

Now, like a detective summoned from bed with bleary eyes, I was trying to understand cause and effect, especially in Chris's case. How had he been living? What and who surrounded him? Did anyone really see Chris?

One of my coping mechanisms, historically, was to ensure that my presence created no ripples. The self-respect that I denied myself made me the perfect houseguest. You'd be hard pressed to determine whether I actually slept in that bed upstairs. I arrived with groceries, and beer. I'd cook dinner for all assembled from the ingredients I had brought with me—and then do the dishes. Your dog was going to love me because I gave each one his or her due. Overcompensation meant that intimacy was held at bay. "Wow, that Shaun—what a nice guy, and so easy to be around." The art of deflection—I was adept.

Given this construct, I was taken aback as I learned the rules of (dis)order in that second home that looked out over one of the few tidal rivers in New England. It was very hard for me to imagine how Chris had been able to function in an environment of such deep chaos.

The weekends were a rolling, bacchanalian extravaganza on most occasions. Friday was for the arrival of the guests and light drinking—foreplay. Saturday was for the beach, beer, and baby oil until mid-afternoon, and then the return to home base for the professional cocktail hour, which started at a civilized 3 P.M., depending on the tide and general conditions at the beach. Dinner was timed to coincide with the end of Tom Martin's second bourbon, after a sixth long day of psychiatry counseling in his second, local office. Things were rarely static in that environment.

When I walked in with my arms full of groceries and beer, the refrigerators were already stuffed beyond capacity. Leigh had made that run earlier. Because of my already mentioned modus operandi, it made me feel somewhat off balance and I had barely arrived.

Tom carried a heavy load. Beyond the large rambling old-money house in the better part of Newton ("Top Ten School Systems in the USA!" yelled Time magazine) and this summer home—under expansion—there were four daughters on the verge of both college and marriage, and two practices seventy miles apart from one another, where the soundtrack resonated with tales of incest, pedophilia, depression, and hopelessness.

Understanding this (about his burden) only served to kick my overcompensation into high gear and I just didn't appreciate that it was a breach of protocol when I stood that first night to wash the dishes. The message was that "pitching in"—especially as a male attendee—was just not necessary.

In fact, it was difficult to determine just how to engage with a group that was so incestuously tight—it was a play. Leigh and the young men were at center stage and anyone else was part of the audience. I felt as though I was a member of a different generation entirely, and not just three years older than most of those at the table. I had never felt such separation from Chris, but it was strong in that house. How had Chris operated in this turmoil?

Doctor Martin was normally positioned at the head of the table. He'd have changed into his weekend gear by late in the afternoon on Saturday: red suspenders that lay flat in an oval shape around a broad core that pushed the straps out, to the left and right. Underneath, a soft, tan colored chamois shirt neatly tucked into green Woolrich pants. Standard issue boat shoes provided comfort, and the entire ensemble was a liberation from the suit and tie he wore for half of each twenty-four hour day and the lion's share of most weeks.

During my first night at dinner, all of Chris's closest friends were at the table, as were a trio of Martin daughters, currently living at home. It was a fast-paced game of late-adolescent, male-dominated, one-upmanship and verbal sparring, all to the delight of Leigh Martin, who multi-tasked to cook the dinner and to provide drinks for those with empty glasses. She stood enthralled in dewy-eyed wonder by the rollicking, comforting ritual unfolding before her. The stimulation was compensation for a long week of isolation.

This setting offered such a vastly different canvas than I was accustomed to. In my family, society was avoided. Mom's bout with polio during the depression drove a strident approach to living. She asked for no sympathy and put on her game face each day but disengaged from the larger community around her. Our house was not loud, and to compensate, I seemed to be drawn to friends with large families and lots of action.

Dad was an only child and small. He expected to get beaten up. He kept his fists up to protect his face and once said to me, "In the morning, when I get up, I stand at the top of the stairs for a moment, trying to imagine the most negative things that I'll encounter when I reach the first floor. My hope is that they won't be realized and the day will improve from there."

So, the snap and frenzy in the Martin house was unfamiliar, but something I had yearned for, always. In chaos, I became invisible and the pressure was off. For me, Thanksgiving at their home (to come later) crystallized all that I had imagined about and hoped for in a family much larger and less constrained than my own. Within my family, it was primarily an exercise of avoiding the hot spots.

I sat to Tom Martin's right and as he leaned back in his chair and pulled at the inside of his left nostril, he exaggerated his small town North Carolinian accent and offered an extended, Southern assessment of the proceedings.

"Oh...sheeeeeet!"

He told bad, racist jokes about Chinese dentists who solved patient problems with a diagnosis that "abscess make the farts go Honda."

When Leigh acquired a brace of white Pekin ducks, it fell to Tom to name them after some of his southern childhood friends: Gutterball, Dooney Tickle, Oochie Lewis, Guinea, and Monroe Hale. He accented the first syllable: "MON-roe."

By now, he was starting his third bourbon and his face was perspiring lightly. He leaned closer to me—not conspiratorially, since he made no effort to turn down the volume. He just wanted my full attention.

"Leigh-Leigh is crazy for them fuckin boys!" Then he sat back in the chair, chuckling in appreciation of his commentary, as his suspenders bounced lightly on his smooth chamois shirt and his face became a bit more flushed.

Like the narrator in *Swann's Way*, deprived of his goodnight kiss but transported by a confection, memory seems to be distilled into a few pages of one liners like this one. Big ticket experiences don't always have the resilience that these shorter vignettes have, over the long haul.

A throwaway comment by an over-burdened and slightly shitfaced observer of all things perverse secured a toehold in my memory bank and was destined to resurface, from a distance, in a less chaotic time.

Chapter Eight

Discovery

It was late in November so that when we left my father's house abruptly, after dinner, it was already dark. It was raining very lightly. My car had no wiper delay so I alternated between no wipers at all and their lowest speed, which was too much, although it was a form of distraction. I had not given up on cigarettes yet, but that was on the horizon, and if ever there was a time to step all the way up to Kool, I was on board. So, I cracked the vent window and pushed the lighter in to heat up that round silver coil. About twenty seconds later, it popped out, offering to assist.

Sue was in the passenger seat, staring at the floor. I shook the pack of cigarettes so that one extended through the porthole: an offering, rejected with a short shake of her head. It was probably her hair that first caught my eye months back and now, as the oncoming lights refracted through the raindrops and bounced over her curls, I was suddenly very tired and our first days seemed like a previous life altogether.

"I really didn't need to know this shit," she spoke, quietly, and continued her inspection of the floor mat. Another one liner I'd hear for decades hence and at the most unexpected times.

"I know. I'm sorry."

"Why did you tell me?"

"I'm not sure. I thought you should know. I thought someone..." I did not finish.

"How did you get those letters from my mom?"

"They were inside one of Chris's jackets."

The rain had picked up so that I could leave the wipers on, and given that reality and the end of my cigarette, there was nothing to occupy my hands, which wanted to fidget. We had been drifting apart for a while and after this it was difficult to imagine how we'd ever get the buggy out of the culvert and pointed north again.

My father's house was about halfway between the apartment I still occupied in Newton, west of Boston and Wareham where we had spent the weekend. I'd been seeing Sue since Chris died, which had me in Wareham regularly, and as a result, we'd end up at Dad's for Sunday dinner at least once a month.

I had visited him alone, earlier that week. Shortly after I arrived, I opened the refrigerator in the small pantry directly off the kitchen and pulled out two bottles of Bass Ale. The dew point that day was high and the bottles perspired, profusely. We moved to the living room, breaking our usual pre-dinner routine. I have wondered why since and it does not matter.

The living room had been painted just before my father and stepmother moved into the house—the first they had ever owned—during the same week that Chris had been buried. The walls were the same hue as bluebird eggshells.

There were two large cameos in black frames with a round gold hoop on top of each—for carrying, it seemed, though they were not going anywhere. A green terra cotta umbrella holder sat next to the bottom of the walnut banister that rose to the second floor. In the holder was a collection of canes—various types, none used by anyone in the house, and I could see one standing proud above the others with a gold lion's face on the top plate, which would rest against your palm if used for a stroll. My dad was a collector of weapons of singular destruction so I knew that if you pulled on that piece, it would produce a long, thin sword that could do some damage in a pinch.

"I need to show you something," said my father. I could see an envelope on the side table, next to the Morris chair that he had found at the Morgan Memorial store and had lovingly restored. It was a fine example of American art from the late 19th century and a nod to one of the classes he taught on a regular basis: "American Civilization Through the Arts."

He stood partially, to hand me the envelope, and started to explain as he sat back down. From the kitchen, I could barely hear the radio, tuned to the late afternoon jazz show that Phyllis liked. Tony Bennett was asking to see what Spring was like on Jupiter and Mars.

"Do you recall Christopher's tweed jacket?" he asked. Oftentimes, because of his classroom voice, or his experience in the theatre, his phrasing sounded like something from a courtroom transcript. "Do you recall where you were at approximately 8 P.M. last January 17th?"

I'd have used "remember," not "recall," and for some reason the formality of the question made me shift position to a less comfortable edge of my seat.

"Sure, I know that jacket," I replied.

"Recently, I was moving some things from out of my closet to the attic and I thought it would be a good plan to put that jacket in a proper mothproof garment bag. As I was putting the jacket into the bag, I felt a bulge and discovered this envelope stuffed inside the lining of the coat."

As he was explaining this, his large tiger cat named Harry Lyme brushed against my leg and sprawled himself on the braided rug that separated the two of us. His tail slapped the floor idly. At the same time as I pulled the pages out of the envelope, there was something about the handwriting I could see that was very familiar. Exaggerated loops on ascenders and very large print. Every instance of "I" looked like a drunken "H" toppled on its side. I could see all of this before I had read a word and it struck me that this was Leigh Martin's handwriting. Chris's protector, after our mother fled to Florida.

Christopher –

I've rewritten this four times now. But it is heavy and hard to say–so please be understanding.

First, I have a strict code of being open, especially with those I love and am close to. You have become a very special person in my life. And I have to share–OK!?

I don't want to burden you or turn you away, so I take a very big chance and hope you can handle this–my confession.

I have come to love you in another way– above and beyond being Leigh, friend, etc. I didn't want it to happen, but if I were your age, I would want to be that "one person" you search for. I love so much about you–your compassion, sensitivity, your eyes, your voice, your courage, your body. I can easily forget my age and want to cuddle up next to you. I also want so much to see you happy–so don't worry about my being foolish. I won't.

But I just had to tell you of my struggle (every so often). I love Tom and have nothing but respect for him. But the sixteen years between us takes its toll on me during the last 4-5 years. Even tho, as you said, "my life is finished in terms of searching and moving on." I have the same very strong need to love and be loved. And if you and I were to meet at another time and place–you would be my choice for a man.

My telling you this does not change anything we have or will share–please! I may run or do something strange at times in order to control my aching, but you need not fear or expect *things to be different. I am strong.*

I just had to tell you how strong my feelings are–in hopes we could better understand and preserve the friendship we have.

Please don't hate me. I am sorry (well–not really sorry–it is better to have found and never have than never to find I guess).

God–now I will worry so that this whole thing will upset you and make you think less of me.

Probably won't give it to you.

"I hate that bitch," uttered my father as I looked up from the letter. He had read these four short pages any number of times but I was still trying to get up to speed and wanted to say, "Wait."

Often since Chris died, I found myself working to slow down the onslaught of new discoveries—insights about human behavior, in almost every case.

"Wait, so after my mom had cut and run, leaving Chris on his own, he sought a safe harbor within a community he felt he knew and was betrayed when..." Had I uttered these words? I looked to my father. His face had changed so much in the past year, deeply etched with anger.

I was confused and reeling again and felt exposed, as if I was on stage in a dress rehearsal and had forgotten my lines. Each encounter that was unexpected—Ron's dismissive "couldn't take it," Dean Palmer's lack of empathy, Jim stepping back from my side in favor of spectacle, Chris's surrogate mom behaving poorly—had me groping, impotently, for the script I so desperately wanted.

Harry Lyme gazed at me implacably from behind his large amber eyes, taking it all in.

Chapter Nine

A Day Sailor

In the center of the southeast facade of the Martin house at 199 Sandpiper Lane, not far from the beach, was a little-used front door. Most of the traffic in and out of the house used a slider, underneath the deck on the far left end of the old white farmhouse.

There was a massive slab of granite in front of the door that served as the solitary step and on sunny days it absorbed and retained a significant amount of energy, which I was taking advantage of, one crisp morning in mid-May, a year after Chris had died.

Dale had joined me with a cup of coffee and we chatted aimlessly about the weather and the early returns that the Red Sox were posting.

"Man, the Sox looked incredible last night, didn't they?"

Either of us could have started the conversation that way.

Across the lawn and the dirt road that ran down to the river a few hundred yards to the left, sat a 22-foot daysailer on a trailer that needed a thorough cleaning and some new paint. The boat itself appeared to be in good condition, though it too ought to have had a complete cleanup. The paint below the waterline was blue and faded, with some swabs of white beginning to show through.

"What's the story with that boat? Michael O'Leary owns it, doesn't he?"

"Yeah," said Dale. "It's been here for a while—since before Chris..." he halted mid-stream.

"You ever sail?"

"No, but I always wanted to give it a shot."

"This would be a perfect area, with the river right there."

"It would. Seems like it'd be a great place to practice."

Two slate gray cedar waxwings had been passing berries down a row of friends that made up their flock and had decided to take a break by circling the front yard twice. They took two large dips past the outdoor chimney to our right and landed together on the metal handhold that defined the prow of the boat, flicking their tail feathers almost in unison, for balance.

"I'd love to get out on the water more," I said. "I wonder whether Michael would have any interest in selling the boat?"

"Well, if he did, maybe we could buy it together. What do you think?" asked Dale, his enthusiasm growing and infectious.

"That could be great," I returned. "I don't think either one of us knows what we are doing, though." I smiled.

"I'm betting this could work." Dale, now nodding excitedly, began listing the reasons that it could and would.

"Whoa, whoa, let's not get ahead of ourselves here. First we have to talk to Michael to see if this even makes sense. Do you know where he is these days?"

"No, but Sue or Leigh must know. I'll ask them."

Without a cue, we rose together and ambled across the lawn, and then the dirt road to the side of the trailer. The boat had a substantial keel that was roughly five feet tall and in order to accommodate that, the boat sat high in the trailer—higher than either of our heads. Dale walked around to the far side and we each stepped up on the sidebar of the trailer to get a better view of the inside. We unsnapped the tarp that circled the cuddly and pulled it back toward the mast to expose the cabin.

There was some evidence of chipmunks or mice—too small to sail but happy to ride the winter out, away from the biting winds that blew off the Wareham River. The cabin was roomier than I had imagined and included a table with seats on either side and, beyond, a small but cozy sleeping area. The setup reminded me of the various Volkswagen microbuses I had owned or ridden in over the years.

"All the wood needs to be oiled," I pointed out.

"And that small window on the left has a crack," Dale said.

"Doing the work..." we both said at the same time and laughed.

"That's most of the fun, right?" I said and we reached across and gave each other a high five.

"Okay, we gotta talk to Michael," I said while pulling back my side of the tarp and pressing home the silver snaps that ran in a row and around the corner to the tiller.

Dale finished up his side and we both hopped down, but lingered as we inspected the underside and then stared the twenty-five feet up, to the top of the mast.

"She's pretty."

I nodded my agreement and we walked under the apple tree at the far end of the split rail fence and past the fireplace toward the side door of the house.

* * *

Michael O'Leary was handsome, affable, and quick with a one-liner. Though not small, he was a bit of a leprechaun. He had a twinkle in his eye and a head of light brown curls that made more than one teenage girl swoon. In high school, he was one of those guys who was comfortable and at ease with either gender, unlike some of the adolescent football fanatics I knew who, though smitten with the idea of the opposite sex, were so unsure of themselves that they took an us-versus-them stance.

During the winter, he had a full length, cross-breasted army jacket that fell well below the knees. Anyone I knew who wore Army gear in 1970 opted for the standard field jacket. A risk taker, I remember thinking.

Along the way, he had picked up a black and white hound dog and named him Jareb, who was truly a "contender" as his biblical name suggested. You could sit Jareb as far across the kitchen floor as possible and tell him to wait. Then, channeling Roger Clemens, work through a complete windup from the opposite wall and blast a two-inch piece of pizza crust directly at Jareb's head.

At the last possible moment, he'd snap his jaws closed around the projectile and the pitcher could watch the dog's Adam's apple bob once, to confirm a strike. Jareb never missed: overhand, underhand, sidearm—he never flinched and seemed oblivious to the cheers of the bystanders. Dismissive, even. He was in the zone and focused on the body of Christ.

Jareb had been hit by an MBTA streetcar outside Michael's apartment on Commonwealth Avenue and lost his left rear leg. It seemed to have had absolutely no impact on his lifestyle except when he swam, where he had a tendency to turn clockwise.

It was early in the week after Dale and I had discussed the sailboat, and I sat next to the small telephone table outside my room, while Michael's roommate went to find him.

"Hello?"

"Michael, hi, it's Shaun Deane."

"Shauno! What's up, bud? How are you doing?"

"Good, fine. How about you, how's the pooch?"

"Rubskins? He's a pain in the ass."

"No way," I protested, in defense of the greatest catcher I knew.

"So what's going on?" he asked.

"This is a long shot, but I was in Wareham last weekend and Dale and I were talking and, well, we're wondering if you might have any interest in selling your sailboat. Doesn't seem to be getting much use and well, anyway, that's the deal."

"Yeah, yeah. OK, interesting," he said. "I might be, actually. I just never seem to be able to get to it."

"OK. Well, maybe give it some thought and then we can talk again," I suggested. "I'll give you call next week? I'm going back down to Wareham this weekend so I'll have another look and maybe a few questions, though to be honest, I really don't know much about sailing at all. We are looking at this as a project that the two of us could work on, together."

"OK, man, sounds good. Let's talk next week. Thanks for the call."

Later that same week though, after dinner and a swim at the Brandeis pool, I found a message on my bed that Michael had called, so I rang him back.

"Shauno, hey man. I've been thinking about your call and so yeah, I am interested in selling the boat. I could use the cash and like you said, it's just sitting there."

"Ok, great," I said. "What were you thinking about for price?"

"I don't know, really. Maybe around $2,500?"

Dale and I had done no research and we knew nothing about boats, so this price tag could not be compared to any nautical knowledge. Instead, I had to position it against the most expensive things I had ever bought, which were, indisputably, cars. At the time, I had never spent more than a few hundred dollars for transportation, so the proposed price was high.

Yet, I was managing the estates of both my mother and my brother, so that I was flush with funds that weren't truly mine. But clearly, some portion of them would be, when the dust had settled and all the expenses were paid. More than anything though, I was after an activity: something to really get lost in. The boat offered the additional benefit of camaraderie through the partnership with Dale. So, whether Dale had half of the asking price or not, I was predisposed to pick up the slack. I saw it as an investment in mental health.

"That sounds reasonable, Michael. Let me talk to Dale this weekend and then I'll give you a shout."

Dale was already in Wareham on Saturday when I arrived just after noon. We sat on the deck that looked out over the East branch of the Wareham River toward Elephant Rock, just below Cadman's Neck where the river widens and we could see, clearly, that the tide was going out. It was always a beautiful view and now we could consider that, someday soon, we might actually ply the same waters.

I recapped the conversation I had with Michael just a few days before.

"That's kind of steep," said Dale. "I was thinking maybe a thousand."

"Based on what?" I asked, smiling.

"My checkbook." And he grinned back at me.

"Well, honestly, I don't really care," I explained. "I need something to do and I've got some money kicking around—who knows how long that will be true—and so I'm already nodding my head. I can cover whatever you can't."

Ultimately, we agreed that Dale would post $750 and then, at some point in the future, if things went according to plan, he'd pony up more. It didn't matter to me. I just wanted to move ahead.

Now we could begin to consider the punch list of work that was going to be necessary before we'd ever take her off the trailer.

Later that afternoon, once a few more people had arrived, we got a pickup whiffle ball game started. I had perfected a vicious slider and an acceptable knuckleball that summer and, after the first inning, it was mostly strikeouts with an occasional home run off the roof of the house, to the left of home plate, in front of the outdoor fireplace.

During the seventh inning stretch, Chris's friend Shawn crossed the lawn and offered me a brown bottle of Bass Ale, which was wet from the humidity that rolled up from the river.

"Dale tells me you guys are talking about buying Michael's boat," which, given his inflection, was a question.

"Yeah, we'll probably do that next week, when we get back

to Newton," I said.

Shawn tipped his head back and, in two long pulls, finished off his beer and laid it at his feet.

"Dead soldier," he belched, in summary. "'Nother?" he asked, as he nodded his head at my half-finished cadet.

He was back quickly and picked up where he'd left off.

"Did you know that Chris lent Michael the money to buy that boat?" he asked, matter-of-factly.

"What?"

"So no, I guess? He lent him a thousand bucks to buy it a year or two ago."

Chris had been a scrupulous saver. His only extravagances were the occasional pack of John Player Specials from the tobacconist's shop in Harvard Square or a set of new flights for his medium weight brass darts. Otherwise, it was all squirreled away in the Newton Savings Bank. It didn't surprise me that he had an extra thousand kicking around since he had helped me limp through college with an occasional loan to get my car repaired or to pay a utility bill.

I was no longer present in the discussion and can only guess at what was said next, but I was thunderstruck. Shawn's declaration was simple and seemed to be beyond dispute, yet it opposed all logic—it made no sense at all.

Just after dinner on Tuesday evening, Michael arrived at my apartment to discuss the boat purchase. All four of my windows were open and a warm breeze was blowing lengthwise through the room, lifting the edges of the papers that extended from underneath the faux leather blotter on top of the mahogany desk across from my bed.

"Shauno, hey, what's going on?" Michael asked.

"Not much, really. How about you?" I asked without any enthusiasm.

"Stayin' alive, stayin' alive," he sang in a falsetto. The movie had come out a few months earlier and for all of us who grew up on music that spoke to revolution and social change, this disco shit was a complete affront. So anytime it was criticized, it brought a smile, which we shared, despite my apprehension about where the conversation was headed.

"So! A sailing we will go," he said, turning on the Irish charm as an icebreaker.

I was sitting on the edge of my bed and Michael sat across from me in the Harvard chair I had inherited from Chris's room. I did not respond and spent a long time studying his face for something I still cannot name. Eventually, he cocked his head to the left a bit as my dog does when I ask about going for a walk.

"Michael, I heard that Chris lent you the money to buy this boat," I said, trying hard to keep any heat out of the statement. Or was it a question?

"Yeah, yeah. That's right," he nodded, smiling.

Now my head twisted. We seemed to be in different worlds, entirely.

"And you think this is OK?"

He was confused. "What's OK?" And he shook his head a bit.

I just could not accept that he did not see the conflict, and despite my best efforts, I could feel my face reddening as I leaned forward as my voice rose.

"Well, really, you never repaid my brother the money he lent you and now not only are you trying to sell the boat to the executor of his estate, and brother, but you're adding a premium on top of it." I was nearly yelling by this point.

I could see a glimmer of recognition but just slightly.

"Shauno, whoa, whoa. It's not like that..."

Interrupting, cross-examining now, I leaned in, closer. "No? It's not? Tell me then, what is it like?"

"I, I mean," he shook his head and smiled, trying the charm again—clearly this had worked for him on many occasions. I could imagine him talking his mom out of some form of punishment because "he was so darn cute," but I wasn't having any of it, and now he was recoiling a bit in the large black chair.

"Shauno...Shauno. No, man. I mean, I didn't know." He was looking at me imploringly now. Feeling trapped. That made two of us.

I was losing enthusiasm for the kill, as my respect diminished and a wave of battle fatigue rolled up my legs and my back. I slumped a bit.

"Hey, Shauno, I didn't realize. I can make this work. I can, I don't know, I can...I can give you a pound of pot." He was nodding his head at his sudden insight.

"So I'm supposed to do what? Go out and sell ounces to make this all good?"

"Yeah, yeah." He was enthused and did not seem to understand any of it. The absence of any appreciation for the (lack of) ethics involved was incredible to me, but paled next to his apparent confusion about why I was even upset to begin with. So much of my life to that point had been spent just trying to be seen, to be recognized.

"Michael, just get the fuck out of here. I'm done. This is done."

"Aw man, c'mon now. I'm sorry. We can work this out."

"No, just get out. Go."

He stood and ran his hands through his hair, shook his head, offering more apologies, but by then my back was turned and I was staring out the window on the far wall toward the Massachusetts Turnpike, which ran parallel to Auburn Street about three hundred yards distant. I heard the front door click shut and walked over to the stereo I had inherited from Chris and placed the tone arm down on John Klemmer's *Barefoot Ballet* album. The music had offered solace repeatedly after Chris's death, and as the first notes from his tenor Selmer surged through the room, I curled up on my bed, sideways.

I was deeply disappointed that I'd lost a way to get consumed in a project that would let me escape for a while. Rebirth—

replacing worn parts, polishing the brass fittings, and rubbing oil into thirsty teak had enormous appeal. I saw it as a long-term, focused meditation and an opportunity to get closer to Chris through the promise of a partnership with Dale, and now it was going to be back to business as usual.

I folded a pillow in half under my chin and was asleep before the second track had started.

* * *

Eight years later, in 1986, I was living in Walpole, where we rented the first floor of a farmhouse in which the caretaker and his family lived upstairs. The owner was a retired investment banker and wanted to keep the family farm in active use. My son, Travis, had been born that winter and now, as another Spring had arrived, I stood beside his crib in the bedroom next to ours as I pulled on his blue sleeper for the night. His bath was over, we'd read a story—*Winnie the Pooh and the Blustery Day*—and he gummed his knuckles as I stuffed his chubby legs in to the legs of his pajamas.

"You've got Popeye arms," I told him as his crystalline eyes met mine. "Gonna kick my ass someday." I smiled.

I placed him stomach down in the crib and made sure that the bumper was secure so that no stray limbs could poke out through the prison bars.

"Ok, mister man, night-night. Mom and Dad are right next door if you need a midnight snack or you feel like watching *The Creature from the Black Lagoon*. We live to serve."

He was already breathing rhythmically and I turned the dimmer way down on my way out the door.

Evening ablutions complete, I pulled back the blanket and slid in between the crisp sheets that had been hanging on the outside line all afternoon. I had to get up early so I decided to forego a chapter in the book on my nightstand and flicked off the light.

From the other side of the bed, speaking into her pillow, Kate murmured, "He's OK?"

"He's already asleep," I reported.

"Good," she whispered and rolled over the other way.

I was just drifting off to sleep when the phone—much too loud—jolted me upright as I fumbled the handset out of the cradle.

"Hello?" I croaked and cleared my throat.

"Shaun?" Man, that voice was familiar. "It's Sue." How on earth did she get this number? "Dale gave me your number. I'm sorry to call so late, but I thought you'd want to know that Michael O'Leary and his girlfriend were killed over the weekend."

"Jesus! How?"

"They drowned."

"What? How?"

"You remember that boat he had parked down in Wareham? They were sailing it back from Martha's Vineyard and it capsized. No one really knows anything more."

"Jesus."

"I'm sorry, but I thought you'd want to know."

"Yeah, yes. Thanks," I stammered.

Gingerly, I placed the phone back in its dock and exhaled a long slow breath.

"Whozat?" from Kate.

"An old friend. Died, sailing accident."

"That's awful," she said and adjusted her position again. She didn't know any of these people. Within a few minutes, she was back to sleep as I stared up at the dark ceiling with my fingers locked behind my head.

Shauno.

Michael.

Involuntarily, my head shook side to side every so often.

Travis cooed lightly from the next room.

How could this have happened? By now, I had an innate understanding, and perhaps an underlying sense of foreboding, that hugely unexpected things are possible when least expected.

My flight or fight response was in high gear and sleep was a distant possibility. My heart was racing and I had to check on Travis again, even though it had only been a half hour since I had put him in his crib. His lips were moving, nursing in his sleep, and I slid my feet along the oak floorboards to minimize any noise as I made my way to the kitchen for a cup of tea.

As the water heated up and while I leaned against the counter next to the stove, I considered whether I had any responsibility for Michael's demise. Should I have just sucked it up and moved along with the project? If I had, it seems unlikely that this accident would have happened.

When I last saw Michael, I was fumbling for any string that would help to pull me out of the daily darkness I was stumbling through and it would take a long period of self-abuse before I embraced the structure of family life that Kate represented.

Guilt: my latest food group during these past eight or nine years. I just couldn't see any deceit in my actions though and had to let it go.

As I stood in the farmhouse kitchen on that Thursday night and looked out over the cow paddocks below, a distant and partial lyric from a Dylan song presented itself. Something about "all the while I was alone, the past was close behind."

I pulled a jacket off the hook by the back door and stepped out into the dooryard. A half moon was cresting the tops of the pine tree stand across the road and a dervish of fall leaves skittered the length of the barn to my left.

I stood for a while, breathing deeply and holding each breath for a two-count before heading back in for a final baby check and the promise of some rest.

Chapter Ten

Hush Now

Luis Tiant will be pitching Saturday night. So it'll be Saturday. That works.

That game last fall with Shaun was amazing. The two best pitchers in baseball, head-to-head. Sure, Jim Palmer won 2-0 but man, what a game. In the eighth inning, the crowd chanted "LOOIE-LOOIE" and I swear when he spun on the mound, a few times he was facing the Green Monster full-on. That was wicked.

So yes, Saturday. I'll need to put the car in the garage first. It's in a good spot there around the corner, embedded in the hillside.

But this morning, I need to go see Doctor Bass. I hope there won't be any trouble with the prescription. I really have had trouble sleeping, so hopefully he won't push back.

On the way down the stairs in the Newton house, I ran into Bones.

"Yeah, Chris, how's it goin'?" he asked. He had a way of talking like the guy on Saturday Night Live who says, "Yeah, yeah...that's the ticket."

Everyone keeps asking me that and each time it's like pulling the string on Howdy Doody's neck, making me relive the past few weeks in some way. But not today; things are better.

"Going great!" I said. "Feeling good."

"Really?" said Bones.

"Yeah, feeling good. Hey, I'm running late. I have a doctor

visit. I'll catch you later, OK?"

"Yeah, sure. See you later then."

Make sure you have everything, now. No fuck ups. Jack D? Dalmane? Smokes, of course. Step up to Kool. Duct tape. Keys. My letter. Flashlight.

The game starts soon so there's time to tidy up my room some. I checked this morning and sunset is about 7:45 P.M. So maybe I'll miss the first inning or two.

Then, head down the hill.

The garage is built into the hill and there're pine needles all over the roof. It's a small one. I had to juggle the car in and out a few times so that I could close the door the other day, and now that I'm in here, it's a little damp and the door just barely opens all the way. Good call on the flashlight. Man, it's dark in here!

This has been a good car: a 1970 Nova. I took off the foot extension that Mom used (so that she could drive with her left foot) as soon as I got home from dropping her at the airport and I guess that made it mine, officially.

I haven't really done anything else to it since then. It's got the standard bench seat covered in black vinyl and the basic air conditioning system (crank handles for the windows). When Shaun was living at home, he put an 8-track tape player under the dashboard, but there's no tapes anywhere around.

Anyway, all I need is AM, for WMEX. I like Ned Martin. He's a good announcer.

So, duct tape. Start on the passenger side. This roll is pretty full so there should be plenty. The only tricky part might be the curves, up and over the windows. I'll just use extra there.

Now the driver's side. Getting good at this. Oops, meant to keep the window free so that I could have a smoke or two and crack the window. I guess I can use the vent window okay.

I just hate a car full of smoke.

Get it right first, then I can figure out the vent window. Measure twice, cut once.

What am I doing?

The game is on for crissakes. Jesus! Let's get that tuned in first. Must be the 3rd or 4th inning already...

> **"Bottom of the 3rd inning, with the Red Sox ahead 2-0 and Mike Norris will face the 9th batter as well as the two lead-off hitters at least. Mercy! What a night at Fenway Park. 72 degrees at game time and 22,000 in attendance. Norris wheels and deals...and it's a pop-up over third base that Butch Hobson brings in easily and it's one up, one down."**

I love Ned Martin. "Mercy!" Love that.

What a relief that Dr. Bass was OK with that scrip. He only gave me twenty. Twenty is enough, along with the Jack and, well...

Think I'll have a little Jackie D. right now, as a matter of fact. I like Jack. Old No. 7. Lynchburg, Tennessee. I never went to Tennessee. Farthest south I've been is D.C. on my 9th grade class trip. Maybe next time. Jack D. and a Dalmane to take the edge off. I wonder what sour mash means? Mostly I like beer, but I have to say that there's nothing wrong with the Green Chartreuse that Phyllis breaks out on Sunday nights, after dinner.

> **"And Denny Doyle grounds out to 2nd base and the Sox put three up, three down."**

Dammit. At least we have the meat of the order coming up: Jim "Ed" Rice, Yaz, Boomer, and Pudge. Can't imagine having to pitch to those guys.

Time for a smoke, so crank that vent. Wonder how long it takes to heat up the cigarette lighter? Two Mississippi, Three Mississippi, Four Mississippi, Five...hey, that's pretty quick.

Look at that: when I take a long drag, my whole face lights up, reflected on the windshield. And if I turn my head left and right, you can really see where my hair is starting to recede. Twenty years old? Give me a break. This reminds me of that scene from the Wizard of Oz where the Wicked Witch of the North? West? I can't remember. Anyway, where she's staring into the crystal ball and Glinda appears.

You're out of the woods, you're out of the woods, you're out of the woods.

Couple more Dalmanes I think and a nice slow pull on this pint of old No. 7.

"And now replacing Mike Norris is Stan Bahnsen for the Oakland A's. After this brief station announcement, Bahnsen will face George Scott, who so far tonight has hit into a double play back in the second inning, but had a double in the 4th inning. The Boomer has been making good solid contact during all of this early season."

Boomer—gonna get me a tater. Wonder why he calls home runs taters?

Time for another slug, ya bastard. Take another shot of courage. I don't like The Eagles. Fuck that shit.

"And Rick Miller goes down swinging to end the sixth but the Sox put three more on the board and it's Red Sox 6 and Oakland 1."

Speaking of The Eagles, let's talk about the real shit: Segovia. I scored seat B17 at Symphony Hall last year. Dead center, two rows back. We even made eye contact a few times. Nobody better. Nobody.

Come 'ere, Jack. Help me make it through the night.

Grasmere. The best. Dad wasn't too thrilled when Dale and Craig showed up but things settled down. Besides, they had their own room down the hill and we spent almost every night at the Traveler's Rest. There is nowhere, nowhere, where you can get a better pint of Guinness. I haven't done much hiking in the States but I can't imagine a better hike than Striding Edge on Helvelyn, in the Lake District. Maybe someday get a little cottage here. There, I mean.

'Nuther Dalmane now. Make that two, barkeep. And a splash of Mr. Jack.

So where are we—besides in the fucking dark? Oops, almost spewed that last slug all over the dashboard. No joking around, this is serious. I meant where are we in the GAME, Watson?

"And that should do it for Luis, who has given up two runs in the eighth inning to Sheldon Mallory, the pinch hitter and Larry Murray, the right fielder."

Dalmane, take away my pain, Jack, Jack you got my back.

Fuck, I am buzzed. In a good way.

Gotta get organized. Toss that letter up on the dashboard. Dear Dad and Phyllis. I'm sorry. I can't.

One more Dalmane and another good shot of courage.

Gentleman, start your engines.

This car runs smooth. I just had it tuned up.

Car.

Smooth.

Kools. Love 'em. They had that penguin in the ads. Willie, I think?

"And Burleson just hits a rope to short right field, scoring Scott and Fisk..."

You're out of the woods, you're out of the woods, you're out of the woods.

Dark in here.

"Jim Willoughby now pitching to Earl Williams, the catcher for the Athletics, with one down in the ninth and no one aboard. He peers in for the sign, winds and delivers, and it's a long, long fly ball and that is going to end up on the Turnpike. Mercy!"

No fuck ups.
No.
No.

Chapter Eleven

Alfred

On the flight back from Florida, bringing Mom home and cruising above the eastern seaboard at 35,000 feet above metropolitan D.C., I pushed my seat back a bit and stared up at the ceiling of the Boeing 727. I was a long way from insight and I knew it would take years to understand all that had gone south in my relationship with her. There's no doubt that I gave her a run for her money after she divorced, underscored by a string of minor arrests in high school. I just couldn't seem to get out of my own way.

It would be easy to say that these transgressions were "cries for help." Resorting to risky behavior would become a learned way of life down through the years and might have simply been the result of no adult supervision.

We were moving through some bumpy air; the seat belt sign was illuminated and I closed my eyes and drifted back to Maine and the winter of 1970.

We were unable to get into Michelle's family cabin, just outside of Portland, Maine, on the edge of a body of water that was shaped like ET's finger. Ancient pine trees circled three-quarters of the pond. The windows were locked tight and the doors would not budge. By the time we gave up, the sun was descending over the far western stand of trees and we decided that we ought to head south—if not for home, at least for a place to stay overnight.

At the time, all three of us were juniors in high school, recently licensed and mobile, but completely inexperienced about the issues related to motel rentals and other vagaries of life on the road. Bob and I had known each other since we were seven, but John was new to the group and a friend of Bob's, through one of their mutual high school classes. John was about to have a rough night.

After driving for thirty minutes, we stopped at the Lamplighter Inn, in Saco. Bob registered in the small office at the far end of the parking lot while the two of us waited in the car. We did not fully comprehend the requirement to register *all* parties and that by not doing so we were immediately in some sort of violation status. Bob returned with the key and the three of us made a quick entry to room 133 as the hydraulic closer pulled the door shut behind us.

There was a yellow bedspread on the double bed and it had a fractal pattern, represented as raised dots woven into the material. I sat on the edge of the bed as soon as I had dropped my duffle bag and got to work rolling a joint to break the ice. I was learning about John, quickly. Apparently, he had decided that on this trip, the time was right to try some LSD for the first time. In retrospect, that made a lot of sense since neither Bob nor I had any plans to do so and ought, therefore, to be relatively under control and calm—always a good thing to have some support when stepping off a ledge for the first time. We'd be available to provide a direct link to the real world. The others were discussing the best ways to ingest the material and determined that crushing the small purple tablet and snorting it would be appropriate. That was happening as I finished up with my rolling activities. John had been moved out onto the launch pad and all systems were go.

"Ouch, that stings," he said, as I recall. Although I was no expert, in my limited experience, the entire process of "getting off" on acid always reminded me of an escalator ride. Slowly and deliberately and at something approximating a forty-five-degree angle, reality was left downstairs in the lobby as one climbed to the first floor, the mezzanine, and beyond. And that was always the open question: to which floor will we ascend? Ultimately, it would become clear that this escalator went to the tenth or twelfth floor and then started to descend. That was always my favorite part of the experience. A bit of a "phew!" and a reduction of anxiety, which allowed me to appreciate the feelings and the visuals without the unanswerable question hanging in the air, "Well, how high will I get this time?"

By pulverizing the tablet to powder, I had to assume that John would not be taking that escalator ride at all and would instead be hopping on a high-speed elevator—going up?—that would leapfrog over the acclimatization process and go directly to the heart of Saturday night. While I considered the ramifications of this alternate approach, there came, simultaneously, a very demanding knock on the door.

Aw, shit.

"Saco Police Department! Open the door!" There was nothing ambiguous about the request. I may not have thought that exactly, but I certainly felt it as my stomach dropped and I ran into the bathroom. I had no exit plan and had not been down this road before, but the fight or flight reaction was automatic and instructed me to leave room A and enter room B—and to get away from where I was.

Of course, I must have at least considered flushing the pot down the toilet, but the reality is that I stuffed what I had under the pillow of the bed—the bed, that by all rights should show no signs of use, yet—as I fled to the bathroom. Putting distance between the contraband and me had to have been job number one. Handling it with finesse was an entirely different matter. Looking back, I realize that almost nothing I did at seventeen was handled with finesse.

The police officer who opened the door to the bathroom was very big, very blue. He had some sort of face disfigurement. His right eye either drooped or was "lazy" and there was discoloration on that side of his face as well—perhaps an artifact of polio, like Bob's father had, or a birthmark of sizable proportions.

Then, it was on to the police station. How did we get to the police station? Of course it was in a police cruiser, but I have no memory of that, despite my claim, earlier of a refined memory. Did we ride together or in separate vehicles?

I had never been in a jail cell before and, thankfully, the cell I was in was a "single," so no roommate necessary. It must have had a bed and a toilet, but I have no recollection of sleeping or using the facilities. The cells were arranged in such a way that I could not see either of my two friends, nor could they see anyone else.

I was stretched out on my "bed," on my side, considering what might happen next, whether our parents had been notified, and how that conversation was likely to go. Bob was fully engaged in conversation with me.

I was glad that Bob was here. He had older brothers, so this sort of event would not be new to his folks, and his mother, especially, was kind and I knew she would understand that this was not a matter of corruption or coercion but was a higher than normal degree of horseplay. For me, the predicted reaction was a big unknown. My parents had separated three years before this and because I lived with my mother, I assumed she would get the call. I was not especially worried about the outcome at this point. During this reverie, I heard John start to speak in a quavering voice.

"Ah...B-Bob?" he stammered.

Oh Christ! That's right, he is *tripping*.

"Yes, John," Bob replied in his kind voice, a voice familiar to me after so many years.

"Are...are the walls in your cell moving??"

"No, John. That's the LSD. You are hallucinating."

"Oh," was the very quiet, meek reply. A long pause, then, "Bob?"

"Yes, John?"

"How long will this last?"

"Probably another few hours, for sure."

"Like two or three?"

"Maybe a little longer than that, John." *Yeah*, I thought, *more like ten or twelve*.

About then, the arresting office came to my cell and opened the door, using what looked like a standard issue skeleton key.

"Follow me," he said gruffly. We retraced his steps, avoiding any contact with the others. This must have been intentional. I suppose it would, eventually, raise anxiety to feel completely isolated from the others, but I had a gut feeling that we were in reasonably good shape, without too much to worry about. We ended up in a small room straight out of Dragnet. There was a rectangular desk in the center of the room and two transom windows on the wall opposite the door. One was cracked open about an inch, even though it was mid-January, since the radiator on the wall furthest from the door was belching steam and knocking irregularly as I sat down. Two four-foot florescent fixtures sat dead center over the table and flickered occasionally. The light was harsh and my throat was dry.

"Sit," said the officer, and as I made my move, an immediate correction came on his part: "Not there...there." Already, I had guessed wrong. He sat opposite me and flipped through a series of pages that were housed in a full metal jacket clipboard, with three punch holes at the top of each page. I sat silently, looking at a coffee spot on the table to the right of his left arm that reminded me of a witch flying through the night sky, hat askew and robes flapping behind in the jet wash.

Suddenly, he leaned forward, now about fifteen inches from my face, and, using the full power of his facial disfigurement, demanded, "What's your name?" using something shy of a bellow. The pepper steak sub he probably had was not fully digested because I got a full dose before his question had even been completed.

"Shaun," I replied as I summoned as much arrogance as a 17-year-old suburban kid could muster.

"Shaun" was not the right answer.

"Shaun *what*?" he fairly screamed, or perhaps it was a bona fide belch. Correction: Pepper steak and onions. His lazy right eye rolled counter-clockwise as he cocked his head a bit in the opposite direction. We were in the final scenes of Moby Dick, when Gregory Peck tried vainly to finish off the white whale, whose eye articulated backwards to see who the freeloader on his back was.

"Shaun Deane," I stated, in a bit of a haze because I was realizing as I spoke that at some point soon, John would undergo the same sort of interrogation. John, very high on acid for the first time. *Oooo, boy*, I remember thinking, *this could get ugly, quickly*.

"Why are you in Saco?" was question number two.

I know I should have been terrified, but about this time, everything was beginning to strike me as funny. I mean, that question could have all kinds of answers and it was a real struggle to bypass the witty or sarcastic replies that were coming to mind in a slew as I struggled to explain about a friend's cabin in a very unconvincing way. Of course, I did not want to pull others, not even those present, into this pool of quicksand.

Next, he reached into a brown paper bag and dropped two pieces of evidence on the table. One was a standard issue baggie of marijuana—not even all that much. In addition to the baggie, he placed (harshly) a small bottle of the very same product next to the baggie. This was the material I had taken some time to clean, removing seeds and stems, so that it could be rolled easily. Cleaning things up was always part of the fun for me. The manipulation, the tools of the trade: rolling papers, rolling machines, carrying pouches—there were just so many great choices.

"What is this?" he demanded.

Are you really asking me this? I suppose the appropriate

answer would have been that I had never seen anything like that, but I was already weeks down the road, knowing that we would somehow be liberated, and my confidence was on the rise.

"I believe that is pot, I mean marijuana." I stated. I almost rolled that "ju" with a Spanish inflection, but thought better of it.

"And this?" he asked pointing to the bottle.

"Same stuff," I offered.

"No. Not the same at all," he disagreed as his eye took off again and gave me a "who do you think you're kidding?" look.

"What's the story with your friend there?" He leaned in a bit and turned his head.

"There're two," I reminded him and he smirked.

"A wise ass, yeah? OK, smart guy. The heeb with the glasses and the curly dark hair." Heeb? I don't think that I had ever heard that one before, but like Justice Potter's famous quote from 1964 about "knowing it when he sees it," this was not a term of endearment, and I knew it, but continued to take a middle of the road stance.

"That's John," and quickly corrected myself, "John Gollub."

"Gallop? What the hell kind of..."

"Goll*ub*. Ub. Goll-ub," I instructed.

Officer Mitchell had an uncanny ability to stare directly into the back of one's skull, which at that point he did for at least 15 seconds. He was using his bullshit meter and trying to determine whether I was playing with him.

For a moment, some humanity surfaced, and I recognized him as a kid on the schoolyard, enduring the taunts from the playground bullies about his birthmark, or his weight, and in that moment, I relaxed a bit. I knew that I was in jail and that I was being interrogated. I was glad that I was not in Mississippi or Tennessee, where I'd likely be looking at an extended jail sentence. I was in Maine, and even with my limited experience, I was aware that the stakes were reasonable and that unless something outrageous developed, we were running out the clock, mostly.

Therefore, it did not seem like my worst idea to cooperate a bit more.

"He's, ah...well, he's a..."

"A what? He's a what? A faggot? Is that what he is?"

"No, no, no. Nothing like that. It's just that he's, well, sort of shy, I guess. My friend Bob and I kind of talked him into coming along and well, I don't know much about him really, but that's what it seems like to me. I think he's a bit freaked out, to be honest."

In 1970, "freaked out" was probably not part of Officer Mitchell's lexicon, but he nodded and wrote a sentence or two down before looking up at the clock on the wall.

"You three clowns are going to make this a long night for me," he said while shaking his head.

"Sorry, I'd rather be home too," I replied to another of his smirks.

"OK, let's go," he said, rising.

"We're done?"

"For now. Back to your cell. I have to talk to the others."

Deep breaths, John-Boy.

The rest of the evening was uneventful. It was punctuated by the occasional need that John had to rub the reality touchstone and Bob did an excellent job of providing some calm within John's maelstrom. Bob and I had little to say, since most everything was obvious, and I may have even nailed a few hours of sleep.

The jail was noisy, even though we were the only residents. The antiquated heating system announced the arrival of new steam on track three with four sharp knocks in the overhead pipes and then, within five minutes, a very small hiss—as we used to say, like a nun passing gas in mass—that rose to a level that was hard to talk over and then retreated to silence along the same longitudinal plot line. The sequence occurred about every forty-five minutes or so.

From the outer rooms, I heard an occasional guffaw and, once, the extended low murmur of someone telling an involved story that included three or four characters. The speaker, who was a member of the graveyard shift, changed his voice for each character and, in an unexpected way, it felt like a bedtime story to me.

It had a lulling effect, like those times when my parents would have a costume party and my brother and I would retreat to our room to watch Boris Karloff with some ginger ale and potato chips. After the movie, we'd turn off the light and consider the motivation of various characters while the silence was punctuated by a drunken hoot or an overzealous response to a bad joke.

I had to have gotten at least some sleep because I was startled by the sound of the key in my lock. A new officer, fresh out of the Academy, placed a tray on the stool in my room. Two small boxes of Cheerios, mystery meat of some sort, and a cup of black coffee, and though I did not take mine straight up, I could use some of the milk intended for the cereal.

"Here you go," he said. "Eat up because we're taking you boys up to Alfred, later."

"Who's Alfred?" I asked.

He just smiled, locked the door behind him, and went off to get Bob's tray.

Alfred, it turned out, was a place, not a person. Fifteen miles west of Saco but still in the County of York, it was home to the county jail, that was the town's biggest employer. Like the Army, everything in jail is slow. The transfer process started after breakfast, but there were forms, and the day shift officers had to be brought up to speed. While the logistics of our transfer were worked through, I chatted idly with Bob. We had all been allowed a call to home the previous night and we considered when and who might be coming to pick us up. John's call could not have been fun, and he was working on some jangled sleep, now that his system had purged most of the toxins. It was not until just before noon that the city and county were ready for the handoff and I wondered whether the timing was intended to coincide with the lunch hour.

Picking up three hippies from out of state on drug charges had to have been big news, and once they had Bob and I placed in the back of one police cruiser and John in a second, the small convoy worked its way south, along Main Street, past Deacon's Luncheonette and Faye's Coffee Shop, then out State Route 111 for the short trip to Alfred. No sirens, but the roof lights were active and more than one pedestrian in town made eye contact with me as I looked out the rear window behind the passenger seat and the two police officers in front.

There was something Russian about the landscape surrounding the York County Jail, and the bunker style buildings, while brick, reinforced the feeling. The jail sat on a bluff, encircled by Layman Way. A river to the east provided some biting blasts that drove a few foot-high snow cyclones around the two vehicles. We were in shirtsleeves and my teeth were chattering by the time they had pulled John out of the second car. Inside the lobby, it was clear that the stakes had changed. I still had no real fear, but the overriding impression was cold: wired, reinforced glass and lots more steel than back in Saco.

Processing was straightforward and by 2:30 P.M., we'd been assigned beds on the second tier that ran around three sides of a cavernous gathering area ten feet below us. Bob and I were roommates, and John for the moment was a single in a two-bed cell. There were perhaps twenty cafeteria style tables with attached bench seating in this common eating area and around the periphery were other functional areas: a small commissary, a television set—always on—in another corner, with a few folding chairs surrounding it. It was Saturday and Lucy was describing something very involved to Desi. No one paid it any attention.

It became clear that boredom was what was being served up. In a higher security facility, perhaps inmates got on to a self-improvement plan that would alter what we experienced that weekend, but the overall impression was of killing time. Everyone in county jail was a short timer in some way, destined for someplace else.

There was no incentive to do anything other than play cards, tell jokes, and wait for the next meal, or bed. The others were not hardened and had been caught, mostly for B+Es, domestic assault, or check forging. We were the only three with any sort of drug violation and that made us cool, and unthreatening.

Unlike John, I was able to take a big picture view of the situation and that provided some acceptance, which helped to keep anxiety at bay. I knew, for example, that our actual crime was minor: we hadn't broken anything, we had not hurt anyone, and we had not done anything immoral. It came down to sneaking an extra person into the Lamplighter and possession of a small amount of recreational marijuana. Dad was AWOL on the home front, so any unpleasantness would be restricted to Mom's reaction and that, I knew, was manageable.

After lights out that night, Bob and I, lying on our flat plywood beds, chatted as we had done since we were seven. Like an overnight camp, there were some others who could not seem to settle down and the quiet was punctured by some of their outbursts.

"I don't know, but I've been told, Eskimo pussy is mighty cold!"

A plea: "Charlie. Charlie! I need your little sister's number, man."

Then, a poorly rendered start to "Honky Tonk Women" and that meeting with a gin-soaked barroom queen in Memphis.

We had stopped talking, and I was floating in that place that was neither sleep nor conscious awareness, when someone from the end of the hall screamed as loud as he possibly could for a full five seconds and then burst in to an emphysemic rattle. That brought me to an upright position quickly.

"Christ!" I said to Bob.

"Could be a long evening," Bob replied.

Soon, though, things settled down, and for the rest of the night, sleep was punctuated by the occasional thump of the heating system or the tinkle of someone peeing into an aluminum toilet a few cells away.

Just before noon the next morning, Bob's mother arrived to help us get released and to get Bob's impounded car from the Saco Police Department lot.

I was relieved to see her, and once we left the Saco Police Department, I sat in the front seat of her white Galaxie 500 convertible and John sat in the back seat. As we merged onto I-95 south for the two-hour ride home, with Bob right behind us, Mrs. Abboud turned on the radio and found a national news program. The Chicago Seven defendants had just been released on bail and their attorney, William Kuntsler, was reading a statement to the press, outside the Federal Appeals Court. In Saigon, five Marines had been arrested on charges of murdering eleven South Vietnamese women and children.

It was early in 1970 and this was the first of three arrests for me that year—a year of enormous personal and political upheaval. The heat wafting up from the floor of the car was making me drowsy. Other than to say "thank you" to Mrs. Abboud as we left the jail, John had not uttered a word to either of us. Beyond a few monosyllabic exchanges over the course of the next few months, I never had a conversation with him again.

Chapter Twelve

Paul

I looked up the Connecticut River, which flowed toward me a hundred feet below the area behind the Vernon Hall Assisted Living facility. Some trees had been felled recently, since they represented a threat, and the view had improved dramatically.

I was carrying fifty-three small cans of Fancy Feast cat food to replenish the supply Dad used to beef up Max, the resident cat, who frequented his room.

In the first of two extended voicemails I had received that morning, in the fall of 2016, my father specified precisely which flavors would be most suitable by using his stage voice—now hoarse—to enunciate the label description of the flavors that Max liked best. He spoke haltingly and finished each declaration with the same word.

"Turkey. Giblets. In gravy…Grilled."

"Chicken and Liver. Morsels…Grilled."

"Beef. Feast…Grilled."

Seafood flavors and anything with cheese included did not make the cut because "Max did not like those." It was not a coincidence that my father avoided fish and cheese, and I considered the word for applying human traits to members of other species and inanimate objects. Personification? Anthropomorphism? Either way, I was pretty sure that given the chance, a hungry cat would dive bomb a plate of salmon and tuna chunks…Grilled.

When I was much younger and worked at Food Fair Liquors in Brookline, I used to enjoy using the two-wheeled hand truck to take cases of beer from the delivery truck at the curb through the back door and into the ice chest. The chest had a massive door that included a large push paddle on the inside to prevent lock-ins. The best part on a humid July morning was the blast of 40-degree cold that hit me directly in the forehead each time I brought a new stack of beer cases into the chest.

The effect was reversed at Vernon Hall on the first weekend of November as I pulled the back door toward me. Inside, it was dry and, as usual, about four degrees too hot for me. The heat accentuated the slight odor of urine and institutional carpeting that was vacuumed regularly, but never deeply steam cleaned. *"This place would be brutal for my skin,"* I thought.

Dad had come from a long line of day laborers, seamen, milkmen, and carpenters stretching back to England in the 1500s, ancestors with great names like Ashley Curtis Deane, Harding Snow, and Frank Levi Page. He knew little about his family beyond those he had actually lived with and it was a surprise to both of us whenever I uncovered a detail that began to establish the map. He had never been told, for example, that his father had a sister (Dorothy, his aunt) who died at the age of two from meningitis.

In the same voicemail that I had received earlier that day, he described that he had become shaky and scared as he tried to use his walker to get to breakfast. We were still rebounding from a message he had left me earlier that week. In it, he accused me of refusing dental treatment for my stepmother, Phyllis, which was completely inaccurate and driven by his diminished ability to comprehend complicated new scenarios. Now, it was our first meeting since the exchange earlier in the week.

I could see the front two wheels of the wheelchair my father used protruding from his room, two doors down on the left, and the top of his head, with one liver spot the size of a quarter above his right ear. He had a shock of white hair that was combed straight back from his forehead. He was bending down to check the supply of Feline Greenies that he kept just outside his door on a small white plate he'd lifted from the dining room. A lure for Max to the breakfast inside.

"Hi, Dad."

"Hi. Hey. Hi. Hi, Shaun," he said. There was no question that he knew me, but I had begun to notice that transitions were taking him more time and so there was a bit of scrabbling, conversationally, as he shifted gears.

"I'm in something of a quandary here. I had bad luck this morning. I tried to walk with the walker, as I've been doing for days, and couldn't make it. Couldn't make the turn in the hall. I don't know what's wrong. I could hardly get back to the room and I was shaking. I don't know what the hell is going on!"

We moved inside his room and I took a seat in a grey wicker chair across from him. He was very small in the blue wheelchair I had purchased for him after he broke his shoulder early in the summer. There was a large protrusion in the area around his left front pocket that I thought might be a pair of maladjusted Depends, but then I realized that it had to be his wallet. It was twice as big as mine and must have been uncomfortable, I thought. He used no cash these days and no longer drove, so a wallet was superfluous, but resistance to giving up yet another component of daily life made emotional, if not logical, sense to me.

Once, when he was out for a tour of Back Bay buildings in Boston as part of preparation for a course called "Victorian Boston," he left me in the car, as it idled at the curb. While he snapped a photo across Newbury Street, I could not resist the urge to stretch my left leg out as far as I could to press the gas pedal down, awkwardly and much too hard, so that the engine roared and I pulled my foot back quickly and slid across the seat so that my back was pushed against the armrest of the passenger door.

He was back to the car in seconds, and though I cannot remember anything that was said, I do recall his frightening stare. He looked huge as he got into the driver's seat beside me.

Now he pivoted in his chair, using his feet to twist the chair around to the right so that he could look out the window at the two bird feeders I had set up recently and I considered that if he stood up, he'd barely make my shoulders.

"That one you gave me, on the right there—oh, do they ever love that one," he smiled. "Always empty. They just drain it right down."

In front of the window was a massive oak desk that the maintenance staff had come up with when he moved into the room the previous spring. The craftsmanship was first rate and included some inlaid strips of light maple around the perimeter and about an inch in from the edge.

The desk allowed him to look out on the birds from where he wrote an occasional letter or put together a semi-regular magazine of essays and opinion pieces. The latest issue still hovered around sixty pages but was comprised almost entirely of photographs of cats and dogs and one letter from the editor. Strongly worded, even vitriolic, position papers in favor of Ayn Rand or abortion rights had had their day and now the magazine was a vehicle to let a subscriber base of forty-eight know that he had not yet gone gentle into that good night.

"I called over to Vernon Green and Faye told me that Phyllis had gotten up yesterday and made it to the dining room at 2 o'clock and sat there for a long time, expecting me," he continued.

My stepmother was across the "campus" in the nursing part of the facility. It was very unlikely that she had made it to the dining room unassisted, but I continued to listen as he went on.

"I told her what had happened with me and that I didn't know if I should try to make it over there and Faye said that Phyllis had expected me yesterday and I, well, I, I just don't know what to do. What'll I do? What shall I do? I called you, as usual, for help. I don't know what you can do either. I was shaking terribly. I slept fine. When I got up though, I could hardly button my shirt. My hands were shaking. I was shaking from head to toe. I'm sorry, I really don't want to lay another burden on you."

"Well, Dad, yes. When I got your messages that was my sense—that you were scared. Was it something about Phyllis that got that all going?"

"Yes, sure. It scared me, yes."

"What scared you?"

"I was afraid of what I might see."

"Like what?"

"Well. Well, that she's dying."

The issue of mortality was an abstraction for him. Since he did not accept it, watching her slow decline made him angry. He was not getting what he had expected during this time.

On some Saturday evenings before my brother died, Chris would stop by my apartment with a six-pack of beer and a pizza. Invariably, a few hours later he would bring up an issue about our family—an exploration, a supposition. Just kicking tires. These instances made me squirm. I was fleeing the family in myriad ways and had little interest in getting pulled back in.

It was ironic then to find myself in my brother's shoes with our dad, in his own dorm room of sorts, asking questions that clearly had the same impact on him. The choreography was challenging. I was aware that like a somnambulist, there were milestones in our relationship that I'd bypassed completely. My mom's "hang tough" approach to each new challenge meant that she pushed on despite the circumstances, with no post-game analysis. Making it to my thirties was an endorsement that her plan was viable.

And while Dad could be charming and adroit socially when it served his needs—his Ptolemaic worldview, with him at the center—was a handicap that obstructed any capacity to truly empathize and walk a mile in someone else's shoes. For anyone involved in a relationship with a narcissist, it means that you have to pick your battles and accept that there would be no true win and, at best, only an airing of the concerns, but rarely resolution.

My desire to know had to be balanced with his tolerance for the inquiry and the dementia that was beginning to make itself known. Sometimes when we sat like this, it felt as though I'd inverted an hourglass.

We were still for some moments and looked out on the feeders, where one small finch actively chased off any newcomers.

"Look at that. Spends so much time defending, he never gets any lunch," he observed.

It was even hotter now and I took off the light sweater I had on.

"What happened to Phyllis, Dad?" It was more abrupt than I had intended.

"What do you mean? When?" he asked, and I knew he was thinking about something that must have occurred just that week. The attempt to bind my question in time was a challenge, especially since I was really asking about the sum total of all the impacts she'd experienced, and a few in particular.

"Her niece, Deb, called me a few days ago, looking for an update," I began. "Once we got past the basics, I remembered that she had described Phyllis's 'hard life' and so I asked her what that meant."

Silent, Dad continued to gaze out at the feeders, now empty.

"Dad." He did not turn his head. "She told me that Phyllis had been gang raped when she was seventeen and spent the night in jail, afterwards. Her father had to bail her out, I think."

He shifted in his wheelchair and now looked off at a place on the carpet about two feet in front of his feet.

"I was shocked. I had no idea at all," I said.

I felt that I was tumbling along the cobblestones. When I pulled this cork, what had I expected?

"Dad?"

Now, he turned his head and looked up at me. I had always been taller than him and it felt more pronounced now and his position in the wheelchair made him seem especially vulnerable.

He pulled back his lips on the left side and shook his head slightly, side to side: No. A familiar gesture I'd seen throughout my life. He did not maintain eye contact and looked back out the window. What was I looking for? There was no question of veracity. I felt compelled to say the words though. I had recently become aware of a greeting that is expressed in some African countries—"I see you." I wanted to witness whatever it was that Phyllis had been through.

"She told me more, Dad."

Now he rolled his head as if he had a stiff neck. One complete, clockwise circle.

"Years later, Deb said Phyllis had a brief relationship with some guy and became pregnant. She carried the baby to full term and then gave it up for adoption?" I knew but I was asking.

"Dad?"

Nothing.

"It's true, isn't it?"

He turned back to me slowly. And, as our eyes met, I felt that I could see the accumulated sadness of an entire generation: Chris, my mom, the enormous amount of effort he'd expended to overcome the poverty of East Boston in the early 1930s and the trajectory that propelled him through a Ph.D. Program at Harvard to this very room, in a blue wheelchair, sluicing through the stones and sand of a sixty-year relationship together, in search of any small nugget that would help to make it alright.

October 14, 1967

Paul,

    I do not wish to see you again, therefore,

this note. The children have been told that you will not be back and why. I will, as I promised, contact my lawyer, but you will have to file for the divorce. I don't know what grounds you will use but I'm sure mental cruelty will do it. I have enclosed expenses occurred during the past month.

Please do not be here or plan to be here when I am. We parted as friends, let's keep it that way. I would like your address just in case, because I may need to get in touch with you. I really don't want to see you again. Please respect my wishes.

I loved you for those seventeen years, I love you now, and I'm afraid I always will. Because of that love, I wish you happiness and peace. Happiness you may achieve, peace will be harder to attain.

Good bye, good luck,

Betty

My dearest Judy,

My own heart's lady, with no gainsaying
You shall be always wholly till I die,
In all my fight against every bitter thing.
The voice of reason bids not that I put love by
But love more faithfully.
This is the end for which we two are met.

When I first read this poem twelve years ago,

I didn't know that you existed. You were seventeen and just about to be married probably; I had been married for six years. I lived in a bad house, I had been fired by B.U., I could see little in the future. I discovered the book of poems by Francois Villon. The first two lines were the most beautiful I had ever read. I thought, give me a love that is worth dying for—or better worth living for. My marriage never exalted me; I couldn't see that it ever would. I was right. I said, sometime I will be able to say these lines to someone who already exists.

Everything I ever believed about life is true, Judy, because of you. So let us be lovers forever, all of our lives. Wife and husband, lover and loved one, man and woman, the two halves that together make an endless circle. I love you.

Paul

DINNER MENU

for the

WEDDING

of

Phyllis Horn to *Paul Deane*

at the

WAYSIDE INN

Sudbury, Massachusetts

Sunday, December 20, 1970

Champagne-Dry

Vichyssoise

Breast of Chicken over Ham, Supreme Sauce

Wine-Rose

Wayside Inn Tossed Green Salad

Green Beans with almonds

Glazed carrots

Meringue glace, Strawberries

Cordials-Irish mist

Monday evening, December 21, 1970 (Phyllis Deane, honeymoon diary entry)

"Right now I feel I want to indulge you until your eyes pop." This from Paul after dinner in a beautiful Victorian dining room. I too, want to do the same for him, being wondrously happy with him as I have been for the past eight months. Such a wonderful man is he. A true man at last. Romantic, sentimental, strong, brave, earthy, ethereal, expansive, and even sometimes practical—all the things I need and more. And I do love him so. No questions did I need to ask whether he would fit here or there, whether we would get along, whether I would feel trapped—no questions—it was right and natural. How good to have such a feeling. Now we go out for our walk. Comrades and lovers—both. And to the hilt.

It was only 4:30 P.M. but it was easy to see that it would be dark within the hour. Neither of us had spoken for a while. Like tinnitus that only becomes apparent when your head hits the pillow, I could hear a steady ticking from the clock on the bureau around the corner. Something about the beat made me think of a very slow introduction to The Chambers Brothers song, and soon "Time Has Come Today" entered this brief meditation session.

"Dad, I'm just trying to understand. There's so much I don't know."

"Me too," he said and nodded, lightly.

We'd covered part of the landscape and now that we had, I did not feel any more informed, but something had shifted and I felt better. I was willing to wait for insight.

Dad, I see you.

Max had slipped through the partially opened door and brushed along my right calf.

"Hey, big guy," I said as I looked down at him and he meowed quietly in response.

"Back to bulk up," said Dad. "You wait here, Max, I'll be back."

I stood slowly and placed my hands on the blue vinyl grips on the back of the wheelchair and turned a half circle toward the door. As we left the room, I switched off the overhead light on the wall plate to my right.

"Leave the door open," my father said. "Max doesn't like to be closed in."

Arriving in the dining room, one of the residents was at the grand piano in the far corner playing "Misty" loudly and it added to the cacophony rolling in the room with high ceilings and compromised eardrums. A white board by the entrance said "Menu" at the top in blue erasable marker and then an enthusiastic, "Fish Sticks!" and "Waldorf Salad!" and for dessert? "Moose Tracks!"

As I pushed Dad up to his seat at the table, he looked back over his shoulder at me, shaking his head, and said simply, "Jesus."

Chapter Thirteen

Phyllis

On Valentine's Day, in the dining room at the Vernon Green Nursing Home, it was much too hot. From the stereo cabinet to the right of the floor-to-ceiling flagstone hearth, country music was being served up. George Jones had just finished loving her today and now Merle Haggard was describing with pride that he was an Okie from Muskogee. My right foot was tapping like a metronome; the music was too loud and I could not hear anyone at the table.

My father spoke so softly that you had to lean halfway across the oak table to catch any of his commentary. When we left, later, Patricia suggested that this was another of his narcissistic strategies to have everyone "lean in," placing him at center stage, where he was most important. The point was hard to dispute.

Phyllis hardly ever had her hearing aids in correctly—or had left them back in the room—so communication with her was limited to a few hand sweeps that looked like she was conducting the music or reaching out to twist my nose, or Dad's, in a gesture of endearment. Invariably, she'd make it clear that she had missed one of Dad's recent observations and he'd repeat himself, in an overly loud voice, punctuated with "For Christ's sake, Phyllis!" At that point, she'd usually scowl and shake a balled-up fist at him, as if to say "you're going to get what I gave you, last time."

I crossed the room and asked one of the resident nurses if we could turn the volume down a bit and, as always, my request elicited a very positive response.

"Oh, of course! Absolutely," they'd respond, as though this idea had never been considered before. It was a strange ritual, since the audio level was competing with almost everyone in the room and so it felt like a strategy more than an oversight.

That famous quote from Einstein about relativity always came to mind—a hand on a hot stove for a minute feeling like an hour, and an hour spent with a beautiful woman feeling like a minute. Lunchtime in the Vernon Green dining room stretched on as far as one could see. But then it was over and I unsnapped the bib from behind Phyllis's neck and pushed her wheelchair back down the long, pale green hallway to her room.

She needed assistance to get into and out of bed, so timing was important. I had arrived at the door to her room too soon— there were no nurses in the vicinity, so I positioned her next to the door and explained that we needed to wait until Gary or Annalee could help us out. Immediately, she clutched the side of the doorjamb in an effort to pull herself up and out of her chair.

"Phyllis, no," I said. "You need to wait."

She would have none of it and continued her valiant but vain attempt to elevate, becoming more frustrated and agitated with each try. Gary was back at the nurses' station and could see the commotion and said, "Phyllis, I'm busy for a moment, you're going to have to wait, please." I considered that I might at least get her into her room and closer to her bed while Gary finished off the tasks he was working on, but this ended up being a bad idea since once the landing zone was in sight, she was even more motivated to launch herself out of her chair and onto the low-lying bed.

The jack-in-the-box activity went on for a minute or two, and because she was becoming more vertical with each attempt, I finally had to place my hands on her shoulders as I said, "Phyllis, no. You need to wait for Gary to help us out."

It was as if I had hit her in the side with a Taser and I was not prepared for the intensity of her response. She whipped her head around to the right, locking eyes with me—eyes full of so much anger that I took a step back, as she slammed her fist down on my right hand that was resting on the arm of the wheelchair. Then, like a feral cat, she leaned down, gnashing her teeth just over the back of my hand, making it clear that she was fully prepared to break the skin.

I blurted out, "Phyllis, hey! I'm just trying to help you here," and she immediately picked up my hand and held it to her cheek and then kissed it three or four times, quickly.

"*Holy hell*," I thought.

Gary had arrived and, with a few admonitions, had her out of the chair and into her bed in rapid order. Then, with a light blanket over her hips and a stuffed kitten held tightly to her chest, we were waving goodbye and I was talking about next time.

Walking back along the hallway, past the group opposite the nursing station who stared vacantly at me, mouths agape, I thought of how much I cared about and how little I knew of Phyllis. Clark University had been a treasure trove of opportunity for my dad. Though small in stature, he could command presence in the front of the classroom and his facility with the content— American Civilization, The Transcendentalists, Irish Literature— and the addition of a nicely cropped beard he had added in the late 1960s helped to grease the skids with Judy Rubin as my parent's marriage dissolved, and then, after that white heat expired, with Phyllis, who sat in the front row, to his right.

She'd have been hard to miss, too. When I met her at the start of 1970, their connection made sense to me. It was easy to see the compatibility and the intellectual alignment between the two of them, and she was very attractive and full of zest, and fun. At their new apartment overlooking Cabot Field in Newton, she offered stability that Chris and I both needed, badly. Every Sunday evening, the two of us would join them for dinner—an infusion of soul food that helped to offset the sub-standard fare of the preceding week.

She had an odd way with a phrase and I remember laughing when in the reception line at the Wayside Inn, during their small wedding a year later, she shook my hand and said, "So glad you could come," as if I was an out of town guest. And there were other phrases that traveled for decades, as well: "You're father needs to see you," and on that April night before I returned to my apartment, "Oh, Shaun, if it had ever been you..." That was the one that I understood least and that kicked my survivor's guilt into high gear. It was offered as an expression of love but it felt like a ranking system and I was already struggling with the idea that I should have provided more protection for Chris.

Gift-giving, at Christmas and on birthdays, was like a competitive sport for my father. He spent the entire year assembling a cadre of gifts—mostly books and movies—that were responses to the recipients' most recent interests. It could be overwhelming and suffocating. The underlying motivation was to turn the attention from the birthday boy or girl back to him, the world's most incredible gift-giver. To keep the peace, you had to operate in kind, as Phyllis's niece Deb found out one year.

At Christmas, he decided that her gift was sub-par and made no effort to camouflage his displeasure. It drove a wedge between Phyllis and Deb that lasted a number of years and from which none of the three rebounded completely. Once Deb had recovered from the initial surprise and the rapidity with which she'd become persona non-grata, she pushed back, and when I had stopped by the house one day, Dad dismissed her in absentia once again, complaining that she'd described the relationship between Paul and Phyllis as "co-dependent," which was, at least, a vast understatement. He snorted and said, "Whatever the hell that is supposed to mean."

Yet Deb was on to something fundamental. Phyllis had buried a world of hurt for many years. She was raped, brutally and multiple times—then arrested for it. Welcome to the 1950s. A dozen years later, she became pregnant, carried the baby to full term, and then gave the boy up for adoption. I did not learn of these things until she was well past eighty. She did not marry my father until she was thirty-seven, which was "late" in 1970s, and at the tail end of her biological possibilities.

He, charming, even dashing perhaps, represented the bedrock of stability and possibility. After burying her potential for year upon year, it was spring and she had been awakened. With Paul, she wanted, desperately, to resolve the past and to start a family anew, but he demurred. The inconvenience, the fact that he'd already "done that," took the possibility off the table and then the shit really hit the fan.

Chris's death dashed all hope—hope of resolving her earlier trauma and then the ultimate irony was that his death (and though my father never would have admitted it, Betty's as well) made Dad the focal point of their still new marriage journey as she held on during the descent into bitterness and hibernation.

It was from Phyllis that I first heard the phrase (she claimed from Eugene O'Neill) that "every morning, I wake up with this damn thing called hope."

The changes the next decade brought were profound. As I tried to claw my way up the slippery bricks of the well walls to sunlight, Paul and Phyllis turned inward. They locked the doors to the outside world—almost literally—hiding behind the darkness that the downed trees in the backyard and drawn shades provided. Their robust list of friends shriveled and the long-standing social ritual of Saturday night dinners with guests were now solo affairs, shared with thirteen indoor cats. Phyllis turned to academia in pursuit of an advanced degree in Greek History as her wardrobe changed from long flowing skirts and bangle belts to tweeds and hair piled on top of her head in a bun.

The mystery and excitement from the time when I had discovered an exotic bottle of absinthe in Phyllis's desk drawer while I was house sitting was receding rapidly in the rear-view mirror. As I continued down the hall of the nursing home to the dining room, I considered that whenever I had called their house—before they ended up here—I would almost always get Phyllis on the line. We'd exchange pleasantries, but she'd quickly turn the conversation, asking, "Want to speak to your father?" When I said once that, "No, it would be nice to talk to you for a while," there was not much to say and I wished that there had been since there was so much unsaid.

Back in the dining room, Patricia had helped my father on with his jacket, and he had a cheap black watch cap pulled down over his ears in anticipation of the push back through the light sleet to the Assisted Living wing, on the other side of the parking lot. As I leaned into the handles on the back of the wheelchair to get some momentum established for the final incline, a cat bolted from behind the small shack where the staff would retreat for an occasional smoke.

"Ah! There's old Max," said Dad. "He'll be ready for some Fancy Feast now."

"Grilled," I offered.

"Yes, he does love that stuff."

I hit the automatic door button on the right wall and waited as the reinforced steel door swung slowly open, lurching six inches at a time, and then I pushed the chair up and over the threshold and into the hallway to his room.

Chapter Fourteen

1982 – Part I

A light snow was blowing down Spring Street toward the Irish Ale House, across the VFW Parkway. The wind was at my back and as I looked to my right, I could see mist rising from my shoulders, warmed by the effort of a long run after work along the greenbelt system that connected Dedham to the city of Boston. "The Shitty of Bahstin," as an old friend used to say after a few beers, channeling Mayor Kevin White.

It was Wednesday, so that meant my second longest run of the week as I prepared for my first Boston Marathon, now only ten weeks out. After I joined the West Roxbury Track Club, I'd been able to purchase a brand new Bill Rodgers running suit and I was feeling like a bad ass as I slowed to a walk, stopped my watch, and loosened my collar. It was the first technical sporting gear I had ever owned and I was still learning about what to wear underneath so that I could hit the Goldilocks sweet spot of not too hot and not too cold. This evening, I had dialed it in nicely and, though warm, I was barely perspiring.

Pushing open the short chain link fence gate, I walked to the front porch and stopped on the bottom stair so that I could stretch my calves a bit before heading inside. The two-story house sat directly across from the V.A. Hospital, where I walked my dogs most days. Recently, the hospital maintenance crew had erected new towers in the parking lots and the amber klieg lights washed the entire backside of the facility in sepia.

A fresh start. During the previous summer, both my job and my latest relationship went south. Yet I was fortunate to have friends watching out for my better interests, so that by September, I had a new job lined up and a sizable apartment just ten minutes away from work. I was able to make it home for lunch to make a quick sandwich while I let the dogs out in the small side yard. The logistics were working, but the first months had been rough as I explored what it meant to meet my great loneliness.

My bedroom faced the street and sat just above an MBTA bus stop where the driver used to have his first coffee of the day, as the bus belched out diesel fuel that was held in check, below the level of my second floor window, by the high humidity in June, after I moved in. I was almost always awake before the bus arrived, and after work, I would resume my watch position in a torpor that lasted all summer. There was little difference between the grey of dusk or dawn.

After the shrapnel from the emotional concussion grenades had been swept away, I had tried to jump start too many things in tandem: a clumsy attempt at a relationship that was available but ill-considered, a trip to Europe with no master plan, a fast track to teacher certification because hell, it was in the DNA, so it must be right.

I was not a gifted elementary school teacher and I had been offered an escape clause when non-tenured slots were eliminated in the school system I'd joined, just north of Fall River. As I stared out over Spring Street like Dr. T.J. Eckleberg, I had no capacity to accept that insight. I was only "doing the needful," as a friend from New Delhi sometimes described drudgery. My ashram was my crow's nest over the first stop on City Route 524.

The front hallway was chilly and I touched the radiator to my right, briefly, to confirm that it was not just the cold trailing in from behind me. No heat, the chill was real. Although I could not hear them yet, I knew that on the other side of the door on the second landing above, my two dogs stood side-by-side with heads cocked, tails wagging in unison.

I had to push my way through the excitement and two wet noses offered to my right palm as I pulled the key back out of the door lock with my left hand.

"Hi, guys. I'm back. That wasn't too long, right? You both okay?"

They were, especially since in our daily ritual, dinner was next on the agenda. I turned right, through the living room and past the shelves of vinyl record albums, supported by cinder block shelves, into the kitchen on the back end of the apartment. Jack Johnson stared at me from the end of the pile. A tribute from Miles Davis. "Right Off" could be next up on the turntable, I considered.

The kitchen had been updated in knotty pine and felt disconnected from the rest of the apartment—like a camp cabin in Northern New England. On the shelf that rimmed the entire room, a foot down from the ceiling, I was working on a collection of international beer bottles. My only rule was "no duplicates," so it was going to take a long time to complete the project.

To support the effort, I opened the dull white, slope shouldered Amana refrigerator door and pulled a Jamaican Red Stripe from the cardboard holder on the top shelf.

"Yah mon!" I said to Billy, a small brown springer spaniel mix with some short dreadlocks behind his ears.

The dogs hadn't understood the joke, apparently, and looked to each other and then me in obvious anxiety; perhaps this would be the day I'd forget about dinner. As I placed the Red Stripe on the counter and reached under the cabinet for their food, the tails began to wag again just as the phone at the end of the counter rang.

"Yellow," I said, expecting a familiar voice.

"Is this Shaun?"

"It is."

"Shaun, it's Jim Carney, on Gould Street—next street over."

"Oh, hi."

"I'm calling because I noticed that the bulkhead doors to your basement are open. The light has been on for the past couple days and it looks like someone forgot to close it up. I called Peter but haven't heard back. It can't be doing much for your heating bills."

"OK, Jim. I'll close it up, thanks a lot."

"You bet, see you later."

Peter Hart was my landlord and lived on the first floor with his mother. He was a draftsman and worked in the Prudential Building on Boylston Street. We didn't see each other often, although sometimes I had run into his mom on the front porch during the summer, when she'd wish me Merry Christmas and I'd escort her back in to her apartment.

I walked back to my bedroom at the opposite end of the apartment so that I could take my running gear off, and while I was changing, I noticed a half finished joint in an ashtray on my desk. I had a brief "should I/shouldn't I?" moment and decided that since I'd just run ten miles at a seven-minute clip, I was by all means entitled to a small reward. Impressed by the amount of smoke I exhaled after the first hit I took, I determined that a second was necessary in the interest of scientific comparison. Once dressed, I had a nice little buzz going.

Pulling my jacket from the back of the chair at my desk, I yelled out to the dogs that I'd be right back and could hear their tags banging against the aluminum bowls, so I knew they would be occupied for a while longer, and as I stepped back down the fourteen steps to the front door, I pulled up the zipper on my down jacket. It felt much colder outside and the wind had picked up and was blowing from the open hospital grounds across the street. *From the northwest*, I thought, as I tromped through the crusty snow on the right side of the house, toward the bulkhead door. Still playing Jeremiah Dixon, I looked to my right—the southwest—and decided that although I did not know him, Jim Carney must live in that small white cape house, since it offered an unobstructed view of the side of our house.

For a brief moment, I thought I saw someone in his window and had an urge to wave, but it was cold and I had no gloves on.

A shaft of yellow light spilled across the yard from the bulkhead doors, a telltale, pointing back over to Jim's house.

"*Fucking A*," I thought, "*it's seriously cold out here.*" To confirm, I blew out a long breath and considered that it looked almost identical to the smokescreen I'd emitted just moments before in the comfort of my bedroom.

I had stepped over the threshold and onto the first of three steps down when I saw the soles of Peter's black boots, heels resting on the final stair. His left foot fell out at a forty-five-degree angle and his right foot was perpendicular to the step—straight up.

I inhaled sharply but continued inside, stooping a bit to get inside of the doorway completely. When I was able to stand erect again, it was obvious what had occurred. Peter must have had a heart attack and when they say "he was dead before he hit the ground," they were not kidding, in this case.

He had spun around backwards and had fallen on his back. On the way down, he must have grabbed for handholds on either side, because a chaotic pile of rakes and shovels was lying across his thighs and his chest. Remarkably, his glasses—the type that had a frame on top and were rimless on the bottom and screamed "1955"—were still perfectly positioned on his nose, though his eyes were open as wide as I had ever seen anyone's to be, saying, "So this is it?"

"Oh God, Peter..." I said, looking up and around and then back to his face. As I did so, my neck emitted a loud stress crack. I started to head back outside again involuntarily – what to do, what to do? And then came back to his side as my body shuddered in the dank basement air. "911," I said and I know it was aloud.

Both of Peter's hands were chest high with fingers curled around an invisible barbell, as if he'd completed the first part of a clean and jerk move, but all I could think of was the horror movie Nosferatu, since the golem had both the wide eyes and curled fingers I could see directly in front of me.

Each time I exhaled, the condensation formed a micro-cloud around my head and face so that all I could see became muted for a moment and then, like a print in a tray of developer, the image would slowly clarify. Although we lived on a busy artery, the only sound I could hear was a slight ticking from back in the basement someplace. Perhaps a water heater.

"Peter. Shit, man. God."

911.

After I'd made the call, a fire engine was across the end of our driveway in just a few minutes. The red dome light ran slowly along the right side of our house, then scampered across the width of the backyard and steadily back down the left side of the tiny white house to the right of us. I was standing in the snow, back from and to the left of the bulkhead opening. My hood was up, and with my peripheral vision curtailed, I didn't see that Jim Carney was now standing to my left and slightly behind me.

"Shaun..."

"Jesus! Aw. Scared the shit outta me!"

"Sorry. Sorry. Jim. Jim Carney."

"Jim. You made me jump there. Sorry, too."

"What happened?"

"I don't really know, but it looks like Peter had a bad heart attack."

"Dead?'

"Oh definitely. Yes, he must've..."

At that point, I could see two of the firemen step back from either side of the bulkhead door. The basement light was dimmed, momentarily, and then a large black boot with yellow piping around the top edge stepped out, heavily, into the small puddle just outside the door. I felt that time was in a state of suspension. Back in high school as neophytes, and in order to figure out classic blues riffs from old 45rpm records, we would play them at 33rpm in an effort to keep up, and I felt exactly like that now, in some sort of full body braking system.

Next came the helmet. It was white but buffed with some black scuffmarks, as if a hockey puck or two had graced the sides of the chief's head. Front and center was the large gold emblem of the Boston Fire Department, and as his trailing leg stepped over the rotting wooden riser and he came to a fully erect posture, all I could think of was Godzilla.

He was illuminated from behind and the red dome light from the truck now flashed across his face every second or two. He was massive. And like that star of the Tokusatu films, there was something amphibious about him: scaly skin, an anthropomorphic torso with muscular arms, and though he had no spikes on his back, they shared a furrowed brow that spoke to the myriad atrocities they had lived and that pissants like me could only experience as a spectator.

Chief Olson looked neither left nor right, and after looking past us to the hospital grounds beyond, he glanced down at his boots for a moment, then raised his helmet back up and in a voice that spoke to a pack-a-day habit snarled, "Nah. He's stiff."

It was an oddly reassuring summary of current events. His commentary was not disrespectful but carried the matter-of-fact assessment that came from thirty years on the front lines and an awareness that, without summary, we could not move on to next steps. Jim and I stepped aside and as he trudged across the backyard and out to Engine 81, I could feel the ground shake slightly. Sometimes Godzilla is benevolent.

To no one in particular, I said, "I left some water boiling on the stove."

"I should get back, too," Jim said as he looked at his feet and shook his head. "What a shame."

"I really didn't know Peter very well..." I started and since I didn't know where that thought was headed, it seemed enough and I stopped.

I don't remember Jim leaving, yet suddenly I was on my own. The chief was on the radio back at the curb and I was having difficulty regulating my body temperature, as head-to-toe shivers alternated with waves of heat that had me opening and closing the zipper on my jacket in an unconscious auto-reflex.

While I looked down at the trail of boot impressions that ran to the bulkhead door, strobe-like images of deceased people looped through my memory: my grandmother in an open casket when I was thirteen and then, inevitably, Chris and Mom in their respective cars, in the garage, in the dark and all alone. Grandma, Chris, Mom, Peter. Grandma, Chris, Mom, Peter. I had to shake my head to make the loop stop.

As I walked back through the gate in front of the house, the chief approached me.

"He live alone?"

"No, he lived with his mother."

"So where's she?"

"I, I really don't know," I stammered, "I've only seen her a few times. I don't know much."

"Shit." Another summation. "Well, let's see what's happening, then."

I looked back over to the house and I could see a gurney, covered in a white sheet, next to the rescue truck. His hands, I wondered, and an involuntary shiver worked my spine.

I followed the Chief through the front door and past the stairway that ran up to my apartment. As he stood, poised to knock on Peter's door, I had to take a step back to see him completely. With his helmet still on, the large standard issue black boots and the amber colored overcoat, he obliterated any view of the door. I was surprised at how light his touch was, as he knocked one-two-three-four at shoulder height.

"Hello? Boston Fire Department, ma'am. Anyone home?"

We stood quietly for ten seconds or so.

The radio mounted to his epaulet hissed suddenly and then a matter-of-fact male voice with a strong city accent came through.

"Four five, code ten at the Horace James Circle."

I counted the seconds before a reply came back. One Mississippi, two Mississippi, three...

"Four five, roger." *Maybe two and a half seconds*, I thought.

"Hello? Anyone home?"

The Chief tried the polished grey knob and the door swung open to the right, stopped by a tall mahogany coat rack with three claw and ball feet. I recognized Peter's blue windbreaker on the peg that faced the living room. I'd never been in this part of the house before. The layout of this unit was different than mine and reversed the positions of the bedrooms. Like mine, though, the kitchen was in back and we were halfway there and still no sign of Mrs. Hart.

"Hello?" Again from the chief.

And now, a response.

"Peter?"

"No, ma'am, Boston Fire Department."

It was dark in the kitchen. The black and grey Formica table was pushed against the opposite wall with a simple straight-backed chair at either end. Mrs. Hart was tiny in the chair to the left. Her left elbow was resting on the table and she fiddled with the drawstring to her nightgown, just below her neck. A short gooseneck lamp that sat in the center of the table and back against the wall provided the only illumination in the large room. The red dome light from the fire truck outside was beating, beating and lighting up the left side of her face.

"I'm afraid I don't have any money," she said. "Are you collecting for the kids?"

"No, ma'am, we're just checking to make sure you're alright."

"Well, I'm fine, but I *am* getting hungry," she said and as she looked up at me, I could see her right eye glistening slightly.

"Is there something I can get you?" I tried.

"Oh, I'd love a lobster and a Manhattan," she exclaimed.

The chief looked over at me impassively.

"Well, I'm not sure about that," I said, "but maybe I can come up with something you'd like."

As I scanned the room, I saw that there was a large silver chain wrapped around the entire refrigerator with a fist-sized padlock connecting two of the links, through the door handle.

"Why is there a chain here?" I asked as I tugged on it, lightly.

"Oh, well, Peter says I rummage through the refrigerator when he is at work, so he put that on."

"*Getting weird in here*," I thought and again caught the eye of the chief.

Bending slightly, and looking directly at her, he asked, "Ma'am, do you have any other children nearby? Other than Peter, I mean?"

"Well, I really couldn't say," she replied and smiled sweetly.

The chief caught my eye and with a nod of his head toward the front of the house, indicated that he wanted a word.

"We'll be right back, dear," he said.

"Oh, that's lovely," she said, now beaming.

Once we were back by the front door, Chief Olson said, "I need to get Social Services in here to take care of her. Might take a while for them to arrive. You don't need to stay, one of my guys will."

"Ok, I don't mind, though."

"Well, it's really a legal issue, but the Social Services folks might have some questions for you."

"That's fine, but I really don't know much of anything," I said, wishing I did, for her sake.

Later on, the commotion died down. Peter had been taken away, and once the woman from the Department of Social Services arrived, it was only an hour or two before she arranged some accommodation for his mother and I could hear Mrs. Hart chattering lightly and laughing outside her apartment in the foyer at the bottom of the stairs and the reassuring low tones of the woman whose name I never got, sounding like a mourning dove as I sat at my desk in the room above them.

Outside, the sharp exhale of the air brakes as the MBTA bus headed downtown, through Roslindale and Hyde Park. Even with my storm windows down, I could hear the scrape of the rubber door gasket as the driver swung the door closed for last call and then the drone of the diesel engine as the bus pulled away from the curve and tried tried tried to make it into second gear for two blocks and finally, after a hurried orgasm, a post-coital hum to the red light, three blocks distant.

I knew, when I got into my bed, with the house now empty, that I was not tired enough to find sleep immediately. The events of the evening still had me jangled, so I worked through a meditation where I simply noted the sounds around me as they came and left consciousness, trying hard not to analyze or assess. *Just let them come and then let them go*, I thought. And then, *Grandma, Chris, Mom, Peter*, as I wondered if some part of my destiny was intertwined with unanticipated shocks like these deaths I had experienced.

From his bed by my desk, Billy, the brown springer spaniel stray who had camped on my back door step the previous year, refusing to leave until invited to stay, let out two short huffs as a couple walked along the sidewalk below.

"It's okay, shush."

From the kitchen, the compressor in the old refrigerator shut down. It was always unexpected when it did so and I supposed it was because the background noise was at a decibel level that was just below noticeable. And then the surprise of the blossoming quiet. That peace was abruptly shattered by the irregular clanging of my other dog's tags against her silver water bowl as she slurped a few last sips and then shuffled her arthritic ten-year-old body down the corridor to the blanket next to Billy.

With my arms crossed behind my head, cataloguing the sounds of a one-hundred-year-old house shutting down for another evening, I had the awareness that something in the underlying hum of the house had changed. Things were different now. Different again, from the perspective of the house that had seen so many arrivals and departures along the way.

Though I had very little contact with the Harts since I had moved in during the previous summer, now I was the single resident and the future was ill defined. A simple consideration in the dark as I rolled to my left side, facing away from the window—and a major understatement about my trajectory. I could not have known that at the time, and despite the turmoil of the previous half-decade, I was poised to embark upon a new period, one of self-flagellation that would drive me to a precipice where only two choices could be made. But that is obvious, I suppose, as all precipices have only two options. And with that, I reached out to the night table and snapped off the small halogen reading light.

1982 – Part II

I had dealt with the deaths in my own family in a chronological way only and had not been able to make connections or to think in a meaningful way about the reasons behind any of the actions.

When I discovered Peter on the basement floor, leaving me as an orphan in that house, it marked the beginning of a period of enormous confusion. I was caught between living for the moment and working to establish a modus operandi that could pull me out of the reactionary place I'd been in since Chris had died and on to a trajectory that I could own, fully.

A wet nose found its way under the covers to my right hand and was nudging it, softly.

"Uh. Gimme few."

I squinted at the clock and was surprised to see that it was after nine and closer to the bottom of the hour. As I shuffled across the old oak floor toward the bathroom, I flicked the power button on the Sony boom box on the bookcase next to the door. It had two lines of red LEDs, one for each speaker, and they lit up in response to the volume of the song underway. When I brought the radio to work one day, David Murphy took one look and exclaimed, "Oh, Deane-o man, them lights are bad as shit!" and I knew I had arrived.

As I continued my journey out of the bedroom, John C. Mellencamp was singing a little ditty about Jack and Diane.

After Chris died, I got involved in a host of activities that seem to have been intended to present validation to an inattentive and uninvolved audience I thought was watching my every move—a series of life affirming endeavors to offset the police blotters that described in matter-of-fact terms that half of my family did not give a flying fuck.

I took courses at the New England School of Photography and then bought all of the equipment needed to build a black and white darkroom at the apartment in West Newton. I enrolled in an accelerated program to become a certified elementary school teacher and finished ahead of schedule. I quit smoking and started to run at the local high school track.

Running was the gift that had staying power. For the next thirty years, it offered solace and was a refuge from all that pursued me. After the jumper cables had been removed from the studs on the side of my neck in 1977, I was already running, though it would be a year or two before my body caught up. When it did, though, equilibrium prevailed.

On the streets, the "busy mind" of the Zen beginner was quieted and I was able to escape for a short while with great predictability. I became obsessively protective of this retreat, and soon my weekly schedule was crafted to serve the running and with only slight awareness of the reason behind it—my mental health.

The interplay between pleasure and pain, the schizophrenia of abuse and reward, and the extent to which this aerobic pounding could function as an antidote looked like one big Skinner box from a distance. Writing these words from forty years down the road, I can see the chaotic yin-yang, the ping pong of self-abuse and self-worship. Work the maze, hit your head, push the button, get a reward.

This was, and is, how I have held the grieving process at bay. By filling the hours, I did not allow everything to seep in. I had not managed the transition from shock to self-flagellation very well. Just because things have calmed down does not mean they have been resolved, and when the quiet sneaks in, it's an opportunity to absorb the complete body blow. My awareness that was acute and while I talked a good game, my practice s abysmal.

Run a casual half marathon, hit the gym for an hour, and at night, I'd snort a gram or two of cocaine and drive my orcycle too fast, head down, my chest almost touching the gas tank as I filleted the darkness to either side and leaned into a sweeping incline to the right.

Sunday was for recovery. Prince Bolkonski was trying to get it on with Mademoiselle Bourienne and I was on the down slope of the longest book I had ever read. A pattern had developed and was, perhaps, self-protective in nature. As I surveyed each upcoming day, I would block out and protect two sacred hours: one for the run and one for the book. Ever since I had stopped smoking and started running, I could hang my hat on at least these two accomplishments for that day. An attempt at salvation, as I worked to establish order in the universe after the Big Bang.

Like the prince, a mademoiselle was vying for my attention, and just to keep things interesting, she reported to me at the computer graphics firm where we both worked. I hardly noticed Cathy when she first started at the company in the print room next to the office I shared with David Murphy, but outside the Boy on a Dolphin restaurant after an impromptu lunch with the print shop crew and four Heineken darks rolling around in my gut, she grabbed my arm and stuck her tongue halfway down my throat.

After that, I was paying attention.

For me, and for many of my generation, classic dating never really took hold. You were in close proximity to someone, for some unspecified amount of time, then a little tinder, a small spark, and then you were "going out." I bent the rules with Cathy though. Perhaps the age difference of ten years caused me to formalize the process a bit.

She told me that she was a big fan of the Memphis Rockabilly Band so when, just a few days after the Dolphin dejeuner, I saw that the band was playing at the Tam, in Brookline, the deal was sealed.

Since I had only seen her in our shared work context, standing beside an offset press that was twelve feet long, cigarette dangling from her left hand as she watched over the reproduction of the two hundred and fifty page *RGS Programmer's Guide*, I was unprepared for what was coming next as I walked from my burgundy colored Malibu with the Batman sticker in the rear window to the front door of the Levittown style bungalow in Needham, behind the Town Yard.

Just as I finished my third rap, the door swung open quickly, and created a momentary vacuum inversion, toward the mudroom inside. A small lamp on a Shaker table beneath a round mirror of black walnut illuminated Cathy from behind. She was dressed entirely in black, starting with some velvet covered pumps I had a hard time looking away from, up some very long legs encased in black spandex, to her torso layered with a tight fitting, long-sleeved shirt with some gold filigree across the bodice, all wrapped with a black lace shawl.

Her hair, also black, which I had only seen pulled back tightly at work and gelled, now fell from a simple part in the middle of her forehead and cascaded down past her shoulders in a cacophony of waves and curls. It seemed as though she had grown eight inches since I saw her earlier that day.

"Hi," she said quietly, cocking her head to the left in a quick shrug as if to say, "Geez, I could hardly get myself together," and smiling shyly. I can't remember that I had anything meaningful to offer and almost certainly gulped. I was invited in and spent ten minutes playing with her small Lhasa Apso called Tribbles while her mother interviewed me about my family. It was in my favor that all of my mother's clan hailed from Northern Ireland, since Cathy's parents were both emigrants from the Auld Sod, too.

Then we were leaving and her mother was sprinkling holy water on us as we stepped outside. I looked at Cathy with a "really?" look, but she did not seem to think it was remarkable other than to say, "Aw, Mom, c'mon."

"Cati. Cati, now when will you be home?"

"Don't wait up, Ma. Not early."

"You be good now, Cati. Do you hear me?"

"Yeah, yeah, geesh, gimme a break." And she looked at me apologetically while shaking those curls.

Outside, I opened the passenger door for her, and as I climbed into the driver's side, she slid closer across the vinyl seat and asked, "Do I look alright?"

"Is this a trick question?" I replied and she smiled as she pushed in my lighter, underneath the radio, and I accelerated away from the curb.

Much later, on the way to drop Cathy off at home, I stopped by my apartment to pick up the dogs, who had suffered mightily since I left. It was still warm out and we had all the windows down—Irish air conditioning. As we dipped through pockets of mist down toward Route 128 and into Needham, with Gary U.S. Bonds singing about this little girl, each of the dogs had staked out one of the rear windows. From behind me came snorts of approval as we left the city behind.

It was past 2:00 A.M. when we rolled to a stop in front of her house and I turned the key off. As the engine ticked while cooling, Cathy slid closer and we were talking quietly about the music and the impending work day—now just a few hours away. I had my arm around her shoulders and she was smoking a final cigarette, turning her head to the right occasionally to blow a billow of smoke out of the passenger window and as it crawled up and over the roof of the car, I thought of Carl Sandberg's poem and little cat's feet.

As she crushed the head of the cigarette out in the ashtray, she leaned closer, just as Billy launched himself toward the passenger window snarling and snapping his jaws as he barked, which got Sly going, too. Inside the car, even with the windows down, it felt like someone had ignited a package of firecrackers.

"Jesus! What the fuck?" My heart was pounding.

"Mom! What are you doing?"

"Cati! Cati! Now you come in this instant. It's late. Come in now!"

Her mother did not seem to be fazed by the implication that she had almost been bitten and now had her head fully inside the passenger window.

"Mom! Stop!"

Cathy turned to look at me.

"Welcome to the family."

And now turning back to her mother, she said, "Go inside, Mom. I'm coming. Go!"

Her mom retreated, uttering something in Gaelic as Cathy slid back across the seat and wrapped her arms around my neck.

"Now where were we?"

I started to laugh since it was about the least romantic moment and segue I could possibly imagine.

"We were at the point where I was heading home to sleep," I said.

"No!"

"Um, yes?"

"No. Don't worry about her. She's wacko."

"We'll just pick it up tomorrow," I suggested.

"Now you're mad," she pouted.

In that instant, I felt the chasm of our ten-year difference. I was a much older twenty-eight these days, and despite her spandex and curls, she was a very young eighteen and I felt like I did when Susie Cunningham burst out of my basement in fifth grade, yelling to anyone within earshot that I'd just kissed her.

And, not for the first time that year, I told myself, "This is nuts."

As we headed into autumn, I was giving myself a good beating. At least two nights a week, I'd be out with Cathy at clubs like The Tam or the recently opened Spit, on Landsdowne Street. Now, anytime I hear "Tainted Love," I am transported back to a short walk from the bar that was packed three deep with a Bass in one hand and a Mudslide in the other.

Although I would cut myself off well before midnight, we'd

normally stay until last call, and with the half hour drive back to the suburbs and an hour of groping and panting, I'd never make it to bed before 3:30 with reveille at 7:00. By necessity, the following night would be early-to-bed and then it was back on the carousel again.

It had become spring and I was watching the late news on Wednesday evening. The U.S. Embassy in Beirut was bombed that day. Separately, President Reagan was describing Russia as the evil empire. An hour later and flat on my back, I squinted across the room to the poster on the opposite wall painted by Frederic Remington called "The Fall of the Cowboy." The quiet in the painting had appealed to me, though the message was not uplifting.

The nocturnal floggings continued. The daily penance of pounding the pavement remained an unorthodox touchstone of sorts. There was a shower at my new job and I took to running along the Charles River at lunchtime, as a way to make the day more efficient. At one point, as I passed through Central Square, a car cut me off at a traffic light and I slapped the rear quarter panel to let the driver know that I had at least some power.

Forty-five minutes later, I was using my one phone call to connect with an office mate to let him know I'd been detained and would be late getting back to work. The car I had hit was driven by a Cambridge Police detective and he believed a cooling off period was in order. I spent two hours with a speed freak who was compelled to scream "AC/DC" at the top of his lungs while kicking the cell door every few minutes. After two court dates and some hefty legal fees, I walked away with the annual Turkey Award from the West Roxbury Track Club the following November. All was not lost.

But meanwhile, I was working diligently to corrupt and crush any intimate relationships of promise. By hurting them, or being callous, I made it easier for others to leave and confirmed my world-view that I was unreachable in every instance. As

I continued to court a very young Cathy, I was writing letters weekly to Debbie, who was hiking the Pacific Crest Trail. The two-thousand-mile hike offered six months to speak openly (in letters) and to develop a closeness that highlighted the emptiness of my pursuit to get laid by Cathy. I knew that, somehow, I'd be ending up with Debbie, yet I continued to chase an orgasm that had been on ice for over a year. Later, I learned that Cathy had been a virgin until that night that she had a friend cover for her while she stayed with me.

I knew that two or three months down the road, the long hike would be over and that would end the endeavor with Cathy, who became, unfortunately, additional collateral damage. My need to conquer outweighed the opportunity to finesse a transition and to offer up some kindness. I had no skills, only a churning confusion that enveloped me.

Once Debbie arrived, it took three months for me to see that there just was not a sufficient level of chaos available. Deep, deep down, the awareness that she could care for me, accept me, and help me was terrifying. I told myself (and her—not well) that she was too ethereal, that I needed definition.

The extent to which that mindset was off the mark was borne out by the recurring image I had of her afterwards, and that I can summon up still, as she walked toward me early one morning from the bedroom, through the living room where I met her halfway as I returned from the kitchen.

She wore a pale green nightshirt that fell to mid-thigh against her shapely long legs, and along the slight V-neck were small, embroidered flowers of pink and blue. Her long Scandinavian blonde hair fell past her shoulders and she squinted through slits still encrusted by sleep but smiled as she curled into my arms as I twisted one of the small flowers between my thumb and index finger, slowly. A hug that went on for decades and a measurement of all that had been lost until Patricia, thirty years later, when it had become safe to take a risk.

Chapter Fifteen

Kate

I met Kate at a summer barbecue, where Bob was living in a large rambling mansion on West Newton hill, in the summer of 1984. He was riding out his lease for the month of August, until the house we were planning to rent in Auburndale became available after Labor Day. Intuitively, I knew I needed society and camaraderie, as I had ended my tenure in West Roxbury and convinced myself that I was incapable of sustaining a viable relationship with a woman. I was single again and leading what was, for me, a monastic existence that was drug and female free, and the additional sleep was driving my marathon training in the right direction.

All that I can recall from that evening is the comfort I got from my lengthy talk with Kate. Yes, it was oppressively humid and certainly there were mosquitos that chased us from the picnic table to the side porch, where the slightest breeze that slithered over Chestnut Street and down Highland Avenue tickled the small wind chimes that hung outside a room on the second floor, above us. I cannot recall what either of us was wearing, or how I arrived, or even any of the other people who were present (beyond Bob and his brother Rick).

The conversation was the first I had been able to have in the years since Chris had died with someone who understood— so therefore, little needed to be said. Kate had returned to New England from Colorado, where she had moved to start up a regional health management organization that was growing rapidly. Just before the previous Christmas, she was summoned home because her younger sister had been killed by a gunshot to the head. The details were sketchy. There was a case to be made for the boyfriend and other possibilities were not off the table, either, though none of that mattered much.

Her father had worked actively with more than one private investigator to unearth the truth, but the combination of dead ends and exorbitant expenses led the family to an ambiguous acceptance. Kate felt compelled to be available to her parents as she stuffed her own pain and this was the first data point that felt familiar to me.

When she asked the inevitable questions I always got, I was able to respond with more energy and eye contact than I'd been able to summon previously. She knows. Here is an oasis.

Then, after three hours that felt like minutes only, it was clear that the event was winding down. The dinner had been cleared and the outdoor furniture pushed back to provide a thoroughfare across the lawn, toward the driveway. Brother Rick was hovering and offering Kate a ride home. It was too fantastic for me to assume that she was not spoken for, and Rick seemed to be the obvious placeholder. I missed any signal that I would have been an entirely acceptable chauffeur, too, and it was a few months before I saw Kate again. As she smiled and waved goodbye before crossing the lawn to Rick's car, my hair was still blown back. We'd had a conversation that was an exchange of facts and comparative experiences and commiserations, but it was the underlying, unspoken acknowledgment of shared trauma that reverberated most for me.

The following New Year's Night, I got a call from Nick, who was living in Lexington at the time. His wife Marcia and Kate had worked together in a mental health facility west of Boston in the early 1980s.

"What are you doing? Why don't you come over? Kate's

here…" This from Nick.

And then I was in Nick's kitchen just a mile from the site of The Shot Heard Round the World. I gave Kate a ride home a few hours after that and on the large granite steps outside her condominium in Charlestown, just shy of another Revolutionary site, we had our first kiss as an unexpected blast of icy drizzle blew the hair back off her left ear lobe to expose a simple diamond stud.

On the way home, heading west on Memorial Drive, I emerged from under the Longfellow Bridge and yelled, incredulous, into the cold night, "Don't tell me I'm going to be happy?!"

The rush to check off all the boxes on my "Now What?" list, driven by my compulsion for normalcy, did not feel desperate to me. The pace was breathtaking, though, and despite my statement on page one that ambiguity was my foe, there is a distinct haze that covers the first year we spent together. A few months later, as we walked back to Kate's car from the Harvard Square Theatre on the uneven cobblestones that lined Brattle Street, I was struck by how much different she was from anyone I had been romantically close to before. At the same time, a concurrent awareness that we'd be married ran in parallel and I ejected a simple, "Huh!" and realized that it had not been to myself.

When she turned her head to seek clarification and as I took in her jet-black hair and her strong, pointed chin atop the red wool jacket with a black velvet collar, I felt as though I was in Russia for a moment, with a slightly haughty Anna Karenina. I had signed on the dotted line for all that was promised— marriage, mortgage, kids, a home—and I was leapfrogging over the getting to know you part. It doesn't take a certification in couples therapy (where we landed less than two years later) to see that the distance and inaccessibility I was feeling in an intuitive way was far from "different," or unfamiliar. In fact, it was routine, after three decades in the trenches with Betty.

We were married later that year and then, just 364 days after the ride home from Nick's house, I was following her ambulance to the high-risk pregnancy unit at Brigham and Women's Hospital, where we spent the next six weeks until Travis was born in early February. Sometimes when I look back at the first year or two, and then twenty, I recall a lecture from *The Guns of the Navarone* where Captain Mallory, played by Gregory Peck, excoriates David Niven as a reluctant member of the team that he was in it now—"Up to your neck!"

Much later, as I sifted through my inheritance—a box of costume jewelry from my mother, some desktop effects from Chris, lecture notes, books, and correspondence from Dad—I was stunned by the inherent incompatibility my parents shared. How could they not have seen it, and fled? It wasn't just that they wanted different things, they were simply incapable of offering their partner the essential electrolytes that nurture any viable relationship: acceptance, succor, encouragement—safe harbors. What they withheld was not by design but by default.

And for us, all we needed was all there was to see. For me, structure. I cried out silently for scaffolding to hold chaos and unpredictability at bay and to reassure and offer logic. I was in search of normal. For Kate, it was financial security and a replication of a model that was familiar: Ward and June Cleaver—Dad bouncing down Main Street to catch the 8:05 to the office while Mom stayed behind, creating some havoc at home with a payback due down the line.

Last year, while surveying grapefruit at the local food co-op downtown, I looked up and saw that the young man across the aisle had a t-shirt on that said "You'll Do." It got a smile out of me, and it's an exaggeration to suggest that our relationship was that blunt. There were some tender feelings, but we both approached the union from our heads and less so from our hearts. "This looks right, feels right, ought to be right." Couldn't be right. Then, inevitably, a ping pong match of sorts began.

Themes arose and "helped" to centralize the issues that became fodder for a number of therapists on either side of the country. Parenting styles, our decision—often revisited—to have Kate stay at home, upward mobility and the biggie that arose from these complex challenges: intimacy. When the building blocks to intimacy are riddled with fractures, that dog won't hunt.

The folklore of the dissolution says that I was too soft on the kids, making Kate the disciplinarian. My success in the workforce put her aspirations further and further on the back burner where the heat was higher. Something even more profound kept a wedge in place, though. Kate craned her neck to the horizon, convinced that over the next rise there was bound to be a better story. I had a tendency to drive with my foot on the brake, looking over my shoulder as the landscape rushed by too quickly. As a Taurus, the story of Ferdinand the Bull resonated for me. His desire to smell the flowers and slow the pace was what I had pushed back and, luckily, have been able to reclaim.

"Hurry up."

"Slow down."

These things are not compatible.

When things become vindictive, it's nothing to feel good about. As the brass rings that we each needed escaped our fumbling fingers and receded, we each resorted to behaviors that were familiar but entirely devoid of merit. It was never a problem for Kate to express her attraction to someone else, though we were each monogamous for the duration of the marriage. Reflections back to her soulmate from the time before we met—"He used to ask me to wear a t-shirt, only, in our apartment"—or a recap of the conversation she'd had with my boss over dinner—my boss, for crissakes—about living on a small farm in Provence. Idle musings from her perspective, but it made me feel like the proverbial cat on hot tin.

And for me, the refinement of my rapier wit—the master of the one liner. Able to slice and dice when pushed too far. Like

Ferdinand, when you mess with the bull, you get the horns.

Ultimately, though, it was when our kids went off to boarding school in New England, leaving us in the Bay Area with an empty nest, that our raison d'être had clearly evaporated and the unraveling accelerated. My foot was still on the brake and Kate was straining toward that next town, just beyond the crest of the hill in front of us.

My vacuous attempt to "beat" my parents's record of seventeen years became a pathetic milestone to surpass. To whom did I intend to offer these bragging rights?

Then, it was October of 2004 and I had arranged to meet Kate at Travis's homecoming weekend, in Geneva, New York, where he was a freshman. It was a weekend that served up all that the Northeast had to offer: crisp mornings that left a sheen on the windshield and a search for the ice scraper buried under the driver's seat; a Saturday afternoon football game at McCooey Memorial Field and a sausage topped with sauerkraut; and then, back in the room of the bed and breakfast Kate had rented, an announcement from her that we were going to be divorced— just a few moments before meeting a crew of other parents for a dinner at a pizzeria downtown.

We waited until the Christmas break to tell the kids. I had come up from New Haven on the Wednesday before Christmas and though my daughter Gretchen was home, Travis knew, intuitively, and avoided the situation by staying with friends near Boston and ignoring my phone calls. I was shunted to his voicemail with every try and when we finally spoke, it was an uncomfortably obvious standoff, with him asking me why I needed to come home and my evasion and discomfort only confirming the signals in his gut. Somehow, it brought Gilbert Street back to mind and the vision I had of Jim, edging along the low hedgerow—just before I got the memo about Chris.

You can be waist-deep in the big muddy and see none of it and then, in the quiet of any otherwise ordinary day, it's as if the haze of glaucoma has removed all confusion—why did I not hit Ron? Why did I not confront Jim? And now, why was it me, delivering the news, when it was Kate pushing "go"? Dad disappeared, at least I was present.

The kitchen connected to an informal dining area that looked out over the backyard. The round oak table nestled into the bay window, had ball and claw feet below a central pedestal. The glass of wine in front of me sat on a cardboard coaster from the Half Moon Bay Brewing Company and advertised Maverick's Amber Ale. Gretchen was on my right, and Travis was directly across from me, pushed back from the table and looking back over my shoulder to the koi pond that came with the house and that offered a new hobby I wanted nothing to do with.

As I began to speak, it was impossible to shake the Loudan Wainwright song playing underneath it all: "Your mother and I are not getting along, somewhere, somehow something went wrong," and then a description of love as a very deep hole.

It was eerie to be working on auto-pilot: saying the same worn out words that have been uttered in thousands of dining rooms to millions of teenagers. Like a version of the improvisational show *Whose Line Is It Anyway?*, I'd been handed three slips of paper just before I began: "father," "disclosure," and, naturally, "pain." And then I was out of my chair and standing before the footlights at center stage.

At the same time, on track two, all of the things that were never said in my parents's schism were being uttered and I considered what might have been said—should have been said—as I was actually saying them, myself. For a microsecond, I congratulated myself for being adept and functional, until I looked to my right and saw the pool of tears, growing, just beneath Gretchen's face, which rested on her crossed arms atop the surface of the honey colored table top. She was as still as a bird in a shoebox, just after a collision with a picture window—no sobbing, no shaking, and, suddenly, the beseeching tick of the grandfather clock in the next room grew louder.

I reached across and put my hand on her back, feeling the warmth between her shoulder blades. I was a good father but that pool of salt, carbon, and water on the table has been the apotheosis of all that was hoped for early on and all that came to pass. There was no reason to continue. I wrapped up with a banal resolution or two and as we pushed back from the table for some much-needed space and stood, Kate looked to me and said, "Good job, Shaun."

Chapter Sixteen

1985

Shortly before I met Kate, she had purchased a condominium three blocks from the Bunker Hill monument on Breed's Hill, in Charlestown. Breed's Hill is a glacial drumlin—a mound in the shape of a spoon or a partially buried egg. It is best known as the location where in 1775, early in the American Revolutionary War, most of the fighting in the Battle of Bunker Hill took place.

Apart from the monument itself at the top of the hill, the area was mostly residential, and in 1985, like many areas of Boston, was in the midst of gentrification. It was only ten years after Judge Garrity had imposed court-ordered busing, and some of the lingering anger had been redirected to the current round of invaders, who were driving the conversion of triple decker row houses and old factories and changing the ethnic purity of the community and all that was sacred to Townies.

Just a month after Kate moved in, her small red Toyota was stolen. When the police recovered the car, the kids who'd boosted it had scrawled "This will teach you to leave your keys in the car, bitch" across the dashboard. That set up a lengthy dispute with her insurance company.

She had moved in during the fall, just a few months before we started seeing each other, and in the spring, she was "let go" by the medical consulting company she worked for—something about the Director of Human Resources being threatened by an infatuation the lead programmer had with my wife-to-be.

And although I shared a small house in Auburndale with my long-time friend Bob, almost immediately all of my time was spent in the shadow of Breed Hill. The clarity that my new role offered played to my hunch that although Ephesians 2:8-9 states that "*by grace are ye saved through faith; not of works, lest any man should boast,*" I was going to hedge my bets, put the time in, and take up the mantle as primary breadwinner.

When we discovered that Kate was pregnant, we moved the wedding date up and altered the plans for a large event on Cape Cod to a much smaller venue. And for my birthday, I got a union card and a wedding coat...

I worked at Kurzweil Computer Products in Kendall Square at that time, in a converted factory that was in close proximity to MIT and that had been part of the effort to establish the area as mission control for NASA by John Kennedy at the start of the race to put a man on the moon. Lyndon Johnson had been successful in getting the venue changed to Houston, and eventually, Nixon shut down the effort in Cambridge entirely.

Like a downsized version of Silicon Valley, the area was an incubator for many of the best and brightest ideas and people. KCP was the commercial realization of wunderkind Ray Kurzweil and was producing two important products based upon the same hardware and software "engines". The Kurzweil Reading Machine for the Blind enabled those without sight to be able to free themselves from the restrictions of braille and to have textual material read to them by a synthesized voice system. When I started at the company, I was responsible for producing all of the customer and marketing documentation.

In the basement of the old factory building there was a pre-shipping area where machines that had been completed were undergoing their final test procedures before shipment to their new homes.

To fully exercise the fledgling systems, a standardized test document was placed on the glass platen surface of each machine (like a copy machine). For at least twenty-four hours, the systems would run continuously, in an effort to ensure that the embedded software was recognizing the text correctly and that the hardware that moved the optical reader was moving in all X-Y directions properly. This test process was called "burn-in," and the test document resembled a Dick and Jane primer: "The red fox jumped over the low wall."

On one weekend that spring, the lead engineer had replaced the test document with the lyrics from Devo's "Jocko Homo." As I wheeled my bicycle through the basement corridor, past the loading dock doors and toward the test area, I could hear seventeen machines urgently expressing their German angst while hopelessly out of synchronization with one another.

It was the first week of August and the wedding, much smaller now—only a dozen family and a friend for each of us—had been moved to Concord, Massachusetts, near the rude bridge that arched the flood. The ceremony was scheduled for Thursday evening and we'd booked a room at the Bostonian for our wedding night and a honeymoon a month later to drive up the Pacific Coast Highway from San Diego to the Bay Area.

I left work early on Monday and pushed my bicycle through the oppressive humidity along the Charles River, past the Science Museum and back over the Gilmore Bridge and down into Charlestown before the final rise up to Russell Street. There was a small chain linked enclosure to the right of our large Victorian door and that was where I locked my bike. Then I took the six substantial granite steps quickly and finagled the brass doorknob to the left with a slight jiggle. The contractors who had revamped what used to be a single-family home into four freshly painted condominiums had not gotten the final fit and finish exactly right.

Inside 68A, an old brick wall ran the length of the unit from the living room, through the bedroom, behind the bathroom, and along the kitchen to a small bistro deck that overlooked the landlocked backyard below. Hard to imagine a lawnmower being able to turn down there, I considered. I slid the door open to the left and questioned whether this made sense, given the high dew point and the complete absence of any air movement. To compensate, I snapped on the brand new overhead fan and as it spun up to speed, a few pages presented furled corners on the jury-rigged desk along the bricks that were opposite the kitchen appliances.

That desk looked like a typical college dormitory study carrel: a long piece of wood that straddled two grey file cabinets. In this case, it was a massive piece of oak that was unusually thick and over seven feet long. "*Someday*," I thought, "*that piece will have a more permanent installation in a country setting.*" Thinking big.

I sat down at the desk to open the mail I had grabbed on the way in. Mostly bills and nothing for me as the newest tenant in the building. I dropped the junk mail into the small wicker basket at my feet and, as I did, a ragged corner caught my eye. Through the years, I have tried to determine what it was that made me hoist the basket up to the slightly yellowed surface of that gorgeous piece of oak and to extract what I could now see, plainly, was a letter of some sort and in many pieces. On two adjacent pieces, I saw words of portent ("mistake" and "you")— Kate's familiar swirls in light blue. I noticed some inexplicable flutters in my gut.

Robotically, I gathered up a handful of discarded paper and stuffed them into a small paper bag that I pulled out from under the kitchen sink. Something felt urgent to me and I must have had a plan, but I was on auto-pilot, although my heart was beating faster and I could hear what felt like a train platform bell—ding, ding, ding, now arriving on Track 22. A cicada let loose with a buzz that went on for almost ten seconds. Like a shoplifter who hopes to draw no attention, I held the bag at the end of my fully extended right arm and slightly behind my hip flexor as I shuffled through the living room, back out the front door and down the granite steps I had tumbled up just thirty minutes earlier.

Quickening my pace, I rounded the corner from Russell to Walker Street and thought, "*Never noticed that before...Walker Street again, same name as the street I grew up on.*" I was headed to the middle school that separated the set of row houses along Russell Street from Main Street.

The two, single-story school buildings were L shaped and looked out on the basketball court. A covered breezeway connected the buildings and offered protection from the biting winds that blew off Boston Harbor for much of the winter. On that day, as I slid down the brick wall behind me to a cross-legged seat, the concrete under the portico roof was cool to the touch and I ran my index finger along the crevices in the grout that was breaking apart in some spots and easily loosened.

Inverting the paper bag, the scraps of paper dropped noiselessly with a thud before me. Time for a jigsaw puzzle. I still had no idea what I was looking at or why I was doing this, but compulsion was overriding logic. Now I could see that this was a letter because one of the jagged pieces came from the northeast corner and had the words "Monday, August 5th" in the appropriate position. Written today, Sherlock.

Then, from the pile, I pulled out a larger piece on which the existential question had been written: "what am I doing?" It must fit down here, near the bottom, I guessed as I jockeyed pieces into position, rejecting some that were clearly part of a second page. Now a piece from the middle, uneven on all sides, that included the start of a phrase, and the conclusion was obvious: "I feel that I am making a big mist..." I felt a bit like a Las Vegas accountant and that I should have had a green visor and an arm garter for this exercise. There was no sun on this side of the portico but I felt the heat beating me down.

Side by side now, I had two pages that represented the extent of this hidden gem with borders clearly defined so that the exercise accelerated as I was able to dock more and more of the individual scraps into the narrative searing up from the concrete.

The entire event reminded me of writing messages to friends when I was young in which we used lemon juice and toothpicks (as quills) to avoid interception by enemy spies. The envelopes exchanged held what would appear to be blank pages, yet when held closely to an electric light bulb and moved slowly back and forth, the heat would force a chemical reaction to reveal the words that slowly came into view, light brown on the parchment: "Meet me by the brook at 3 P.M.!"

As I sat in the schoolyard, I was only vaguely aware that the light was fading, yet I could read enough to solidify my case:

> *"Dear Jim,"*
>
> *"It's you I have always loved and I want to be with you, just you."*
>
> *"Shaun is a good man but the passion you and I shared is not there."*
>
> *"This is a mistake. I can feel it."*
>
> *"I will love you forever and for always."*

Well then. This changes things up a bit, Commodore. I leaned back against the bricks. If I was still a smoker, I would be stepping up, all the way up to a Kool right about now. I was on track to get married in three days and my fiancée was pregnant. In so many ways, we were only just getting acquainted. And now it seemed that my best aspiration could be only for second chair. What in the fuck have I done? I do not know one damn thing.

I began to have a conversation with someone who wasn't present. "Would you look at this? I mean just when I'd begun to get a little traction and some fundamental appreciation of human behavior, now this. What am I supposed to do? What can I do? Jesus, I'm trapped here."

I looked up to notice that it was as if the backdrop for a hastily produced high school play had been changed. Five people rushing across the stage in a moment of transition and, suddenly, I was in the dusk once again. I scooped up the morning's news and pushed the pieces back into the paper bag as I rose, stretched, and turned to the north.

As I turned right, onto Walker Street, there were more people out. It was just before dinnertime and it had cooled down a lot—at least a degree or two. Approaching me from the top of the street was Danny O'Toole and his great white Labrador, who was straining against his shoulder harness to greet me and keeping Danny back on his heels at a good thirty-degree slant.

"Good boy, Hank, good boy," I said and placed my hands on either side of his massive skull to give his ears a rub.

"Danny," I said. "How goes?"

"Can't complain about it. No one'd listen," he offered.

Hank was staring up at me from a sitting position. A look of awe on his face and a set of roving eyes that went from mine to my front pocket.

"No treats today, big guy, and I am sorry about this oversight. Next time, I promise."

Hank's tail thumped twice on the pavement and though I was four feet away, I could feel the vibration through my loafers.

"Well then, have a good night, Danny—and you too, mister." I clapped Hank's right rear haunch as I pivoted in a circle and started back up the hill.

Right, onto Russell Street, then "second star to the right, and straight on till morning"—Neverland. I could see the small Datsun that Kate's insurance company had provided just down the street. A solitary seagull navigated the narrow causeway, deftly avoiding the telephone wires that crisscrossed the blocks toward the bottom of Breed's Hill. "*A last dumpster run before lockdown,*" I thought.

I stood with my right foot poised on the first step and took a few long, deep breaths of the thick summer air, and then took five more steps up and jiggled the doorknob to the left once again.

Chapter Seventeen

Cars

When I was a teenager, you could start driving with a learner's permit when you turned sixteen. The wait was excruciating. Once, when my mother went to Aruba for a badly needed break after her divorce, it was a Saturday afternoon in September and the keys, well, they were just sitting there. I had not driven anything, ever, but soon I was backing out of our dirt driveway next to the front porch on Walker Street and onto Proctor Street and up Brooks Avenue with my heart racing and a giddy giggle at the back of my throat. It felt good to be bad and I was full of youthful invincibility.

Brooks Avenue offered up Washington Street, a four-lane thoroughfare that bisected Newton and that paralleled the new Massachusetts Turnpike Extension and the railroad tracks for the commuter line that ran from downtown Boston to the western suburbs. Waiting until there was not a car in sight left or right, and lucky that no other car had approached from behind, I took a left turn too fast and had to course correct twice to stay on the right side of the double yellow line. Maybe it was then that I had my first regret and second thought.

Crossing Lowell Avenue, I was headed for Walnut Street and the right-hand turn that would deliver me to the local ice cream and sandwich shop, where I was sure to be seen (the point, after all). Just past the front door of Brigham's, the local ice cream and sandwich shop, I pulled over next to the curb (if a two-foot gap can be considered "next to") and leaned over to roll down the passenger window since Ken Best was standing right there.

Within minutes, there were five other people in the car and I could feel Kathy O'Brien's thigh pressed against mine as she worked the AM radio dial in search of WRKO. Ken was riding in the shotgun seat and there were three others in the back seat. A full load. I pulled the shift lever down toward the floor until it pointed to "D" for "Definitely" and pulled out onto Austin Street, headed for points unplanned.

The cacophony. Even though the windows were down, the serenity of my escape up Brooks Avenue was just a memory. Four teenage girls, all smoking, all laughing and countermanding orders to "turn it up" or to "find a better station, O'Brien!" Ken leaned forward and was shouting to me in front of Kathy—something about football—as I approached the end of the street. At that point, it felt like it was all of them, and then me, the most unlikely chauffeur, with no particular place to go. "*Perhaps a tour of the high school grounds,*" I thought as I turned left on to Lowell Avenue.

Just then, a shriek of laughter from Sue Ball (nicknamed "Panther Sweat" by a middle school friend) that distracted me and caused me to jump the curb with the right front tire, which blew immediately.

"Jesus!" yelled Ken.

"*Wow,*" I thought. "*An awful lot can happen in fifteen minutes.*"

Ken, who knew substantially more about cars than me, was barking out orders as we ker-thumped and wiggled along next to Elmwood Park—a short greenbelt to our right.

"Take a right, take a right!" Ken shouted. "We'll change it over there." He pointed.

I think my blood sugar levels were dropping as everything seemed to slow down and sounds were now muffled and further away. My ability to complete tasks had moved from the "Assumed" column to the "Hopefully" side of the ledger. I needed to take a right onto Highland Avenue so that I could get to the other side of the park and out of the main flow of traffic.

Mom's Rambler American did not have power steering, which may be an apology, but in any event, the turn was executed poorly and I drove straight into the curb on my left, headed directly at the porch of the Highland Heights Nursing Home. The one resident, who was outside in a rocking chair and covered with a red Hudson's Bay point blanket, leaned forward and I thought his dentures were about to make an exit.

All three of the passenger doors opened simultaneously and I remember Ken urging the others to "go, go, GO."

I backed up and off the curb without any difficulty. However, when I tried to complete the right turn to get over in to the safe zone, where the tire could be changed, I could only get the wheels to turn a bit past the center line, and I had to perform a five-point turn in the middle of the street just to get off the main road so that we could inspect the situation.

"You gotta get the car home, man," suggested Ken in a broad understatement. And then he was gone too.

As I surveyed the priorities, tire changing seemed low compared to getting the car back home. The trip from home had been fast. The return voyage was lengthy and my arms were tired from the repeated three- and five-point turns. In the intersection of Lowell Avenue and Washington Street, it took three complete cycles of the traffic lights, with me in the middle like a rodeo clown and six or seven K-turns, to get positioned in the right direction and headed for Walker Street. No police, no blaring horns. A show of community support all around, in retrospect.

Our driver education teacher, Ed Weist, had always encouraged us to "get that picture view," and I certainly had on that Saturday afternoon. And despite the initial setback, most of my employment for the next dozen years consisted of driving.

I worked at a meat market and picked up carcasses of cows in South Boston in a Toyota Land Cruiser. I had to pass a robust background check so that I could meet a Brink's truck in Foxboro to pick up narcotics and then deliver them to pharmacies across the Metropolitan Boston area. I drove sixty-five seat school buses where the certification process included stopping the bus without using the brakes. The instructor, who looked like Ed Harris as flight director in Apollo 13, leaned over my right shoulder—encouraging me, urging me forward, building trust, until the point that he yelled "BRAKE FAILURE!" and then it was on.

I had the five members of The Spinners in my Newton Yellow Cab one evening for a ride to Boston College, where they were scheduled to perform. Five large African-American men crammed in beside me with briefcases on their knees because the trunk on the cab had no lock assembly and could not be opened. One gentleman in the back simply repeated, "Sheeeeet," slowly, every time we took a corner and the other 480 pounds leaned into him. And then, since I thought they were going to see Stevie Wonder, not realizing they were opening for him, I said, "So, going to see Stevie, huh?" And in response, there was another extended "Sheeeet" and a shake of their collective heads.

At seventeen, with six friends, we took two Volkswagen buses in marginal shape on tour through parts of Canada and across the United States, touching down in places like Prairie Rose, Iowa, and on through Yellowstone to Glacier Park where the key lime green bus blew a piston and we were forced to stay in campsite number 34 at Sprague Creek Campground overlooking Lake Macdonald while the shop in Bozeman ordered parts and did the rebuild.

I bought my first pair of cowboy boots in Laramie. Hitchhiking home with Bob after things fell apart in San Francisco, we were warned not to stop in Joplin, Missouri, because they did not take kindly to hippies. We refused ride after ride since the drivers were all headed to Joplin and then, when we finally got a ride that was headed straight through to Saint Louis, the driver decided he was tired and stopped in Joplin anyway. At a pizza shop, when I put my quarter in to play "Ohio," which had just been released, the clientele began to murmur "longhairs," and we decided that discretion was the better part of valor and left.

Later on, Betty and Chris had decided to make cars a talking point, though, and my relationship with vehicles changed profoundly.

After the dust settled in May of 1977, there were things to do. George Carlin did a sketch about houses and how they are simply places to put your stuff while you go out and get more stuff. I wish I had been able to incorporate some of his philosophy as I approached the challenges served up in my newest assignment as executor of two estates. If do-overs were possible, I'd have done something quick and perhaps even dramatic with the two vehicles of mass destruction that had ended up under my purview.

They could have been donated or even ignited. And if I had really thought it through, entering both in a Demolition Derby might have been enormously gratifying. Once again, the guidance I needed so often was nowhere to be found and I could only default to positions that made up the larger, societal belief system in which gas-fired vehicles are revered.

Thus it was that only two months after my first trip to the Sunshine State, I was en route once again, to retrieve my mother's white Plymouth Duster for new duty in the Northeast. The attorney from Newton Corner who was managing the legal affairs of both estates had sent me off with a long To Do list, but once I stepped down the two concrete steps into the garage at 2013 NW 38th Street in Oakland Park, the aperture narrowed and my goal became simply to get the house locked and the car moving up I-95.

The smell of carbon monoxide was overpowering and I gagged as I searched frantically for the power button to open the garage door before realizing that it had to be pulled open manually. When I yanked the handle, hard, it cut the bottom section of my right index finger and then I had to push myself into the bathroom in search of a Band-Aid.

The police had locked the car as part of their close down

procedures, and I had to shake the keys out of the 9"x13" manila envelope I had been given by Detective Arden in April. The door swung open, leaving me little room on that side of the garage, and I had to sidle my way onto the light tan seat. As I put the key into the ignition, I looked down at the seat and saw a very distinct stain, dead center and opposite the radio.

Drool? Vomit? As the garage filled with fumes, I watched Mom slumping to the right since it was hard to imagine she had buckled her seat belt. Then, like a Top 40 song that you just can't shake, that image was looping in the back of my mind and my stomach heaved a bit.

I had never considered the aftermath of a final decision like she'd made and the most obvious first realization was that the car had run out of gas. Excellent. Now I needed to have it towed.

After getting the car back up and running, I pulled out of the station and almost immediately into a small convenience store so that I could stockpile some water and snacks for the trip. I asked for a pack of Kool Milds but they didn't have those, so I got a pack of Old Golds instead. I wasn't smoking that much anymore but on a long trip, the more distractions, the better. I considered the map rack for only a moment but it was a straight shot, I-95 all the way to Route 128. A blast of hot humid air engulfed me as I pushed the door open and walked back to Mom's car.

As I pulled open the driver's door, I noticed a logo next to the word "Duster," just back from the left front wheel. It was a whirling dirt devil topped by a Mexican face with a black handlebar mustache and a sombrero tipped back from his forehead. I named him Tuco, after Eli Wallach, and pushed the air conditioning lever to high while I arranged the new supplies on the front seat.

Traffic was light and the entrance to the interstate was about fourteen traffic lights north, where State Route 870 crossed. As I pulled onto the entrance ramp, I remembered that Bill Robinson, my trail camp counselor from ten years before, had told me that it was a good idea to floor the gas pedal as you entered the highway as a way of clearing off the spark plugs, and as I did, I glanced in the rearview mirror, half expecting and hoping to see billows of bile ejected behind me, but there was nothing except a whine from up front, under the hood. I didn't know it would be true then, but I never saw 2013 NW 38th Street again.

Three and a half hours later, as I passed Daytona Beach, I ran into a huge swarm of crickets that came at me like a hailstorm. At first, a few glanced off the windshield and one left a glob of green goo just to the right of dead center, and as I turned the windshield wipers on, I looked skyward, thanking my patron saint Jason for topping off the washer fluid. Quickly, though, I was in the middle of a cloud of the creatures and had to ease up so that I could see better. The crackling noise from the tarmac underneath the car was so loud that I had to turn up the radio.

By the time I reached New Jersey, my head was nodding and I had had a few mild hallucinations, so I pulled into a space at a rest area, intending to get some sleep. The drone of the highway was relentless, and after an hour with my eyes closed, I shook my head like a Labrador leaving a lake, to tackle the last five hours of the mini Odyssey.

When I pulled up in front of my apartment at mid-morning, I was glad to see that the driveway was empty; everyone was at work. In my room, it was warm, so I pulled the shades down over the open windows and slipped under the sheet as I pushed the light blanket off to the side. I was jittery from the drive and found myself on the verge of sleep repeatedly, and then the Moro reflex would kick in and I'd jolt awake with a sharp intake of breath.

Much later, when I opened my eyes, it was grey and still quiet. Dusk? Dawn? I couldn't tell whether I'd slept eight hours or twenty hours. Either answer was good.

I had stashed the car in an open space to the right of the old garage at my apartment on Auburn Street. Getting it from Fort Lauderdale to Newton in one straight shot was an empty victory.

I walked away with bragging rights that I had driven twenty-four hours solo, but not many awards are given for that. Now, it would be just a matter of finding a buyer to beef up the checking account from Betty's estate a bit.

I didn't drive the car again until Phyllis's friend Helen bought it two months later. Helen was the human resources manager, at the small defense-contracting firm that Phyllis worked at in Needham, and lived just down the street from my Dad and Phyllis in Stoughton. I don't remember anything about the transaction or any of the conversations with Helen, but in an ironic twist of fate, after my non-tenured teaching position in southeastern Massachusetts was eliminated, I took a job as a production editor at the same company—IMLAC—where Helen and Phyllis both worked. It was my first position at a "real" company and when I pulled into the parking lot to begin on a Monday morning in July of 1981, the only available space was directly behind Tuco—the beige Plymouth Duster I had hoped never to see again.

After Chris died, my father decided that it would be useful to have a second car. As it was when he left the family, there was no conversation about the car, his hopes, my concerns—any of it. And, to be honest, I'm not sure I would have been equipped to have a rational conversation about anything other than my To Do list during those halcyon days, which consisted of a very basic set of goals: get up, do stuff, recover—numb myself. It does seem as though we ought to have discussed the implications and what it all meant, though.

Decades later, I am unable to comprehend how my father was able to drive that blue mobile mausoleum from his home, along Route 128 to Bentley College, and back for the next twelve or fifteen years until it rusted away. Was it a tribute? A tangible manifestation that, yes, something had existed and then, perished. See? *See?* Sadly, it could also have been no more complicated than one more example of a depression-era mentality taking the pragmatic approach—stockpiling in times of plenty, for days of want.

I gave him a pass on this and I regret it. My compensatory tendencies to not make waves, to empathize with the guy who'd lost his son. His son, for Christ's sake! Well, that seemed to trump my own losses and kept me silent. For most of the next two decades, though, I was confronted by that Nova every time I visited his house and by that Duster for the few years I worked with Helen. The semi-regular visuals of these weapons created the sort of claustrophobia one might feel along a woodland path when a spider web from the previous evening is encountered.

I gave both a wide berth in the ensuing years, and never, for example, parked behind either one again. Bad luck, after all.

Chapter Eighteen

Congo Cruise

There were still pockets of fog drifting over some of the lower lying greens of the nearby golf course as I drove to the office of my primary care physician, Dr. Ruth Hoddinott. After a tedious meeting at work the day before, I was in the bathroom and noticed that the arteries on my forehead seemed much more pronounced than usual. As a precaution, I had stopped at our small local hospital on the Half Moon Bay coast side on the way home. My blood pressure was elevated and the attending physician, Gary Weiss, who looked like Christopher Reeves as Superman, encouraged me to see my primary care physician for a full "work up," and soon.

It was while driving past the sixth tee that I felt a lurch, as if the road had shifted, and not unlike that feeling when an earthquake begins, though in my experience they all have unique signatures. I squeezed the wheel and straightened my spine. Checking the gauges, pivoting the wheel slightly, and surveying the vehicles in adjacent lanes, I couldn't detect anything wrong with the car.

I noticed that I did not seem to be able to bring in a complete breath, however. It felt as though my belt had been cinched in a few notches. "That's odd," I said (aloud, and it seemed like there was an echo). Now I was paying more attention since, clearly, something was underway. My stomach—always the first subsystem to send out alerts—was active. These were not simple butterflies. Without realizing that there had been a change in my posture, I discovered that my right hand supported my chin and my elbow rested on my right knee—an unusual driving position. I was in the middle lane and, suddenly, I felt very exposed and was compelled to get as far to the right as possible.

There was entirely too much stimulation on all sides. I flipped the rear-view mirror to "nighttime," so that I would not have to be so aware of the tailgater directly behind me and I turned each side view mirror down. It seemed important to narrow the aperture and to focus on getting to my destination, intact. The Kentucky Derby and blinders suddenly made enormous sense to me.

I was reminded of a feeling from a few years before this, as the Loma Prieta earthquake kicked off. I was sitting on the steps of the Apple company store in Cupertino, flipping through a book I had just purchased, when the ground lurched. I had that feeling you get when you have had too much to drink and you know that you're about to vomit. Was I having a stroke? When I looked up, it was clear that terra was not so firma as I watched the street roll by me in two foot swells, much like the ocean in Princeton Harbor near our house, and as the cars bounced around within and almost out of their parking spaces. Then, starting from further down the street, the transformers on the tops of the telephone poles exploded, marching down the street one by one and sending out plumes of black smoke after each report.

Now, I was monitoring every body function closely. There was the same feeling that control had been lost and the basics that we can take for granted—firm ground or the miracle of breathing—could no longer be assumed. My heart was racing, and simple but required movements had become much more difficult. The invisible connection between brain and muscle was weak. Actions that were normally automatic required forethought and deliberate execution. Engaging my directional became an exercise in sequential thought: hand down from chin...thrust arm forward to lever, press up but...get the hand back to the chin immediately! The radio was too loud, but when I adjusted it, the difference was too acute and I had an obsessive compulsive moment or two of adjusting the volume up and down, only to end up where it had been to begin with.

While finagling the radio controls, my eyes must have left the road for a moment since I hit the rumble strip along the breakdown lane. The vehicle-jolting feedback made my heart leap like the scene in Charade when the killer in hiding jumps out at Audrey Hepburn. Now I noticed that my foot was up on the dashboard to the left of the steering wheel. It seemed like a requirement to become more compact but this only served to restrict my breathing more, so I put my leg back down on the floor but that made me feel much too open and, Christ, is that the exit, as I swerved off the highway, cutting off a red Yugo, driven by Barbie with glasses, who raised her middle finger in salute.

Now I was on a left sweeping exit bridge that hovered over all eight lanes of the highway and dumped the traffic down into Daly City like the Congo Ride at Nantasket Beach. No splash down today, except the acid reflux in my gut. The doctor's office was three blocks up on the left-hand corner. It was a nondescript two-story building with parking out back. My face was flushed, my armpits were damp, and I felt that brushing my teeth would be almost as refreshing as a shower.

After I turned the ignition key to "off," the engine ticked slowly—a counterpoint to my own ticker, which was racing. As I extricated myself from the car, I took aim at the main door of the professional building. I'd have to navigate the lot and front walk first and get myself to the second-floor office. I had only been to this facility once before, and now, like Odysseus, the prow of my longboat sought home.

Everything was exaggerated. I shuffled down the sidewalk feeling like Kevin Spacey in The Usual Suspects, lurching and shuffling, but I was also belching and gasping. I had tunnel vision and monomania: get to the door, then get inside. The faded, copper framed front door of the health clinic stuck a bit and when I gave it a good pull, it knocked me off balance as a young mother with two in tow smiled, since she assumed my gesture was gallant, not clumsy, and then gave me a second, questioning look as we passed. As I stepped inside, I got slapped by a blast of warm air that made the walls close in around me, suddenly.

There was an elevator to my left, but in the interest of expediency, I mounted the stairway, which was open on both sides and, typical of buildings crafted in the 1970s, had aggregate steps of concrete with stones embedded for traction. I rode my right hip along the bannister for increased stability all the way to the landing on the second floor. Without a glance at the nameplates, I grasped the doorknob and leaned in with so much gusto that I was propelled from the threshold across the lobby to the reception counter where, without introduction, eyes bulging and hair askew, I bellowed, "DR. HODDINOTT!" A demand, not an inquiry.

The receptionist, unfazed, placed her hand over the mouthpiece of her telephone handset and said, "Dr. Hoddinott's office is on the *first* floor!"

"Ah, gawd," I expelled and then flung myself back out the door and leaned into the railing again and rode the semi-circle back down to the lobby.

Dr. Hoddinott's waiting room was nearly full. At the counter, as I explained that beyond my actual appointment, something else was going on, Dr. Hoddinott approached the desk from an examination room and handed a folder to the receptionist. She looked up from the desk with a smile, turned her head to the right slightly, and asked, "Are you ok?"

"No, I'm not," I stammered and then released a torrent of too much detail capped by a final plea to "get me down, please just give me something to slow things down."

"Let's get Shaun into 2A," she directed the nurse just behind her and, within a minute, I was lying on top of the paper that's always too loud with a cuff on my left bicep and my heart thump-

thumping. As Theresa, the nurse, released the pressure with her index finger, we both looked at the readout on the monitor screen which flashed 160/120 and alternated with my heart rate (98) as she said, simply, "High."

Ruth Hoddinott was no taller than five foot two with thick black hair that was shorter on the left side. Soon the hair on her right side would touch her shoulder. It was hard to imagine that she was an endurance horseback rider, a sport in which riders and mounts competed in fifty and one hundred mile events during which veterinarians checked the condition of the animals every twenty miles or so. She rode an Arabian gelding named Syrah and I could imagine that it must have been an excellent outlet for a busy primary care physician who practiced on the edge of the Silicon Valley.

She treated me (and all of her many patients) with great respect and kindness. At the same time, she had a no bullshit style that worked well for me. She was direct and very thorough. It was obvious that the office was busy on that Tuesday afternoon and I had introduced an unexpected variable by commandeering one of the four examination rooms, but when she knocked twice and entered the room, she was fully present and I'm sure that her kind smile brought my systolic frenzy down a few beats at least.

"This is not the right way to get some time off from work." The smile grew a bit.

"Man, I don't know what the hell is going on," I said.

She asked for and I provided a lifestyle update that went back to our last regular appointment.

Her glasses, with deep blue frames, hung from a lanyard around her neck. The color was good with her hair and she fiddled with the left clasp as she scribbled some notes on the yellow legal sized pad she had brought along with her and tapped the end of her pen against her pursed lips a few times.

"Sounds to me like there's not too much downtime in your life these days. I think what we ought to do is to see how things go here for a while. Let's have you rest for a bit and see how you respond to a break in the action." And then another smile, as she scooped up her notes and put her hand on the doorknob.

"I'll turn these lights down. Take a little nap, I'll be back in a bit."

It did feel good to rest and to close my eyes for a while. When the familiar knock-knock came again, and I looked out through the venetian blinds, the light had changed and I could tell that we were now in the late afternoon.

"How are you doing?" asked Dr. H.

"Better. A lot better"

"Well, let's see if these vital signs agree."

I cocked my head to the right and could see that all of my numbers were down from the peaks I had presented upon arrival.

"Still a bit high but much improved."

As she adjusted the cuff on my arm, she paused for a moment.

"You know," she began, "the neurons in our brains have a finite capacity. Their ability to tolerate stress is high, but not infinite. As we age, the top end, the potential, decreases so that, essentially, our ability to tolerate stress decreases over time. In your case, I think there's been a lot on your plate for a while and now you've heaped on a large second serving and the system is pushing back on the request."

"So what do we need to do?" I asked.

"I think we'll need to monitor your blood pressure, generally— you can buy a monitor for home use, and I can give you a small amount of medication for situational issues like the one you experienced today, but the real answer lies in stress management. You're going to have to get comfortable with an approach that can include self-calming practices throughout the week and on a moment-by-moment basis, when necessary."

It sounded good and right, but I did not know what it all meant and in what way I'd have to make changes.

Later on, I was sitting up on the edge of the examination

table as Dr. Hoddinott wrote a prescription for some Ativan and described that she wanted me to come back in two weeks to take a look at my blood pressure readings from home and to address any issues. She had called home and talked to Kate, so that box was checked.

"Well, Mr. Deane, I think you are all set to go home and get some more rest. Do you feel that you can drive?"

"Oh yeah," I said with some false bluster, "no problem." And then I was free. I was surprised to see that the waiting room was entirely empty and that, apparently, we were the last two in the office. She had stayed longer than she planned, I was sure, and I was grateful to her for that.

As I walked to my car in the now vacant lot, my anxiety scramble into the building was a distant memory. Closing the door to the car and accepting the interior hush, I stared down at the rubber mats and was immediately transported back to my VW microbus, sitting next to Bob as Jim put me on display, almost twenty years before. All of those years with everything and everyone else on the front burners. Now I would need to pay attention to me, and that would be a learning experience since the wall of "Look at me; I'm fine" was thick and had been a central part of my survival strategy for a very long time.

As I turned the ignition over, I had a moment to consider whether I actually *was* okay to drive and dismissed any concern immediately. As I pulled out on to King Drive, headed for Highway 280, I had to adjust all of my mirrors—artifacts from the Congo cruise a few hours before. Soon, I was above Rockaway Beach and I couldn't help but think of the Hunter S. Thompson piece called "The Edge," which described a hair-raising motorcycle ride out of San Francisco and headed to Santa Cruz along this very same road—no helmet, full throttle, and riding The Edge— the demarcation line between those who have "gone over" and those (the living) who pushed control as far as they thought they could handle.

I felt rather pedestrian, in contrast, as I hung back in the right lane, fully enclosed and watching to make sure I didn't exceed the 45 mile-per-hour limit.

"Jesus," I said aloud and shook my head along with a slight smile.

Then, my eyes filled with tears and out loud, again,

"Shit. Christ."

I pulled up the driveway of the house we had moved to just six months before. Now each of my kids had their own bedroom and there was even space for an office. The carport door opened into that office, and as I placed my hand on the doorknob, I was already rehearsing a bit. Kate would care less about what had happened or how I felt—especially my fear—than about what it all implied. Weakness of any sort was unacceptable in her family. I understood that, but it didn't make it go down any easier.

I expected an insincere mercy hug, but then the planning process would begin—how to avoid any disruption to basic services, given my new status. All I wanted to do was to slump into the new leather couch and look across McNee Ranch to Montara Mountain with a glass of crisp Sauvignon Blanc to my right and to think only of whatever moment I was in and how very far I had strayed from what mattered and who I really was. I didn't know anymore. Perhaps the jig was up.

As I swung open the door and stepped in, Luna, our yellow Lab who was really almost white, rushed to me with a green tennis ball in her mouth that pulled her eyes down a bit and she leaned her muscular eighty pounds into my right side.

"There's my good girl," I said, giving her ears a rub as she sighed in appreciation.

Chapter Nineteen

Tiverton

I never did like our house in Rhode Island, especially the second floor, which ran the length of the side that faced Nanaquaket Road, an area named by the Algonquins when their birchbark boats plied the local inlets that led to the Sakonnnet River and out to Newport Bay. The second floor had been redesigned as an accommodation to the aging process with an elevated toilet and an enormous king-sized bed that precluded intimacy.

At the start of the new millennium, doctors, lawyers, and retirees, along with refugees, returned to native New England and worked the landscape in expensive foreign cars. It was 2002 and fifteen years since I'd been a resident of New England.

The move "back East" was something we had discussed repeatedly during our time away, particularly, it seemed, in times of high stress.

Now, I lay on my right side, heavy in the musty, pale blue wall-to-wall carpet in that second-floor bedroom, as my breathing returned to a steady state. My face was pressed to the pile and a smear of tears and mucus covered my right cheek. I didn't care. I didn't wipe it away.

The words I had howled out loud, more than a few times, still hung in the air.

"I want to die. There's too much pain. I want to die! Please, please." Begging for it and not caring about survival, for the first time ever, really. A place I had sworn I would never reach.

No one was home and it was mid-afternoon on Saturday, late in October, but it was an Indian summer and sunbeams lit up a patch of the floor two feet away. Like a hedonistic cat that stretches toward the one perfect spot, I inched closer to some warmth. In so many ways, I had been pulling toward warmth for my entire existence.

As I rolled over onto my back and stared up at the frosty, yellowed globe on the overhead light, I could see at least a half dozen bugs who had been trapped, seeking warmth also. At the same time, I recalled a toy from the bedroom I shared with Chris, on Walker Street.

The Joe Palooka Bop Bag stood proud at roughly four feet tall—eye-to-eye with an average sized eight-year-old boy. Joe was inflatable and had a subtle triangular shape, which made him narrower on top. Down below, he sat upon a double thickness of heavy red plastic that encased a few pounds worth of playground sand.

He had his eye on you. The good eye, anyway. Dapper in black and white boxer trunks that rode just above his knees, he was bare chested. He had well-defined pectorals and his left glove was held back, at sternum level, while his right hand was cocked and at the ready just below his chin.

Black hair swept back from a squared-off forehead and glistened from sweat and pomade, and the cut over his left eyebrow had started to force the eyelid down. It was clear that we had done some damage, but Joe was ready for more.

That was the thing: Joe was always ready for more. Smack that leering face with all your might and, sure, he'd end up on the mat, but the damn sand would have him upright in no time saying, "That's it?"

Whale him on the left ear with a full roundhouse and he'd skitter sideways across the room, but along the way, while sliding, he was already regaining his feet. We stood toe-to-toe in our Keds with Joe Palooka and gave him all we had, and yet he'd never lose his composure and he would always regain the vertical.

As I stared at the ceiling above Nanaquaket Road, I did not feel like Joe. I did not want to get up. I did not want to keep coming at the opposing forces I'd been slugging for the past few decades. Acknowledging that reality terrified me. Like Joe Palooka, I had always been able to rise. I could see and had to accept how profoundly alone I was in that room, in that house, and in that marriage.

I stared at the cards in my hand and saw no royalty. Worse, I could see a history of misplays and impulsive bluffs. This is why the casinos in Vegas have no windows, I understood. When the sun rises, it can be a bit too much.

Years hence, I would read about, consider, and begin to incorporate the notion that attachment causes suffering. On that crisp October Saturday, though, I felt only chagrin and an awareness that I could have been much more self-protective— more self-loving—if I'd acted on the many signals I had been offered since before we said "we do."

Five years into the union with two children under four, I often crested the hill that separated the Silicon Valley from the fog enshrouded Half Moon Bay coastline considering that I would need to get a divorce. And now, I felt embarrassed in some way that my blindness or my willingness to subjugate drove my own present and deep pain. Partly, too, I felt a sense of failure that I had not "pulled the trigger" first. I was as competitive as anyone, and being on the receiving end felt small.

With a long commute to and from New Haven each week, I had many hours to consider chronology and the domino effect, but until this Saturday in October, I had not felt the profound lack of empathy across the borderline that separated partners soon not to be. I told myself that, boy, if the tables were turned, I would at least be kind. Words of solace for someone familiar and floundering. If the tables were turned. If I'd acted first. If I was in charge.

When the subject of my first marriage comes up in my father's presence, he sometimes repeats his own story, where he'd had dinner with his mother a month after he married Betty and expressed his concern that there had been a mistake. My grandmother, Grace, replied that oh yes, well, she had known the same thing about his father on her wedding night. Whenever I heard this story it made me feel as though I was walking through a corridor of cobwebs, again. Those who do not learn from history doomed to repeat and all of that.

Just one year before, I had stayed behind in the Bay Area to wrap up the sale of our home and to supervise the moving company while the thriving start-up company I had joined imploded. I was one of the original, founding employees and though the payroll grew to almost fifteen hundred, I was one of the last ten out the door.

On the weekend before the movers arrived, I was running up Sunshine Valley Road in Moss Beach—the next town over from our house on the coast side. On my right was a large horse property that backed up to the foothills of Montara Mountain, and as I surveyed the brittle fields, a solitary hawk rode the thermals in large counter-clockwise circles as she moved slowly to the north and up the chaparral, beating my eight minute pace, vigilant to the ground below and all without moving a wing. Energy conservation at its finest.

Transfixed so, I almost missed the grey Saab that was headed toward me down the hill, but I heard my name yelled and turned to see that Jan Sommer had pulled her car over and was out and standing near the rear door.

She was a little bit taller than my shoulder and had thick auburn waves of hair that just touched her own shoulders. With the weathered split rail fence on the other side of the culvert as a backdrop, she exuded good health and her eyes sparkled brightly. I felt comfortable in her presence the first time we had met and it was a pleasant surprise to meet her like this, unexpectedly.

We hugged just as a small dirt devil made its way along the fence line beside us, kicking up some dust and a few pebbles so that we both had to look down at our feet. Jan was a therapist in Half Moon Bay and we had met with her a few times during the rockier parts of our marriage. These sessions were tactical and short in duration. Kate continued to see her for a while after we ceased the visits as a couple.

"Well I'm making a new start," she explained "and moving my practice up to Vancouver." Now I was recalling how much I had benefited from her direct communication and her comforting eye contact.

"That sounds great," I offered. "I've heard it's beautiful up that way."

"Oh, yeah." She grinned. "Amazing kayaking and wildlife. This area has just become so expensive. I found I was working so many hours just to make ends meet and then I had no time at all to enjoy the beauty around us. That's dumb!" And she laughed and shook her head. Her eyes twinkled like Santa Claus's and I realized that was one of the reasons I had trusted her early on and so quickly.

"Well, I certainly hear that," I said. "We're moving, too—on our way back East. My job in the city went south and, well, it just seems like a good time to do what we have talked about so often, as you know. Both kids are in boarding school in New England as it is, so it all just seems to make sense."

"What are you going to do back there, Shaun?"

"Well, actually, I'm planning to make a complete break from high technology and with a friend start a business putting on long distance sporting events."

She looked at me directly and said, "Interesting. Well best of luck with that! I do think that is going to put your marriage directly in the crosshairs, though."

She studied me after dropping that nugget.

Momentarily confused, I was on the verge of seeking clarification but then, because of all the time I'd spent in her office and the enlightenment I had enjoyed, I asked, simply, "Because of financial security? Or perhaps lack of?" I smiled.

She nodded and I thought that she might not go further.

"If things are not rock solid, financially, Kate is going to be very, very uncomfortable. Anyway, I want to wish you the best of luck, Shaun. It was wonderful getting to know you and I hope things go really well back there." I wished her the same and knew we would never cross paths again.

As we parted, and I kicked it into low gear for the run up the long grade, I was making plans to test her theory. I needed corroboration, some form of "summing up" that might confirm signals I'd had since before we were married. And I felt a strange sense of excitement and resolve.

Outside, from the yard across the shared driveway, my neighbor had just started up his leaf blower. What an exercise in futility. And with the Earth spinning at a thousand miles an hour, that small patch of sun had now moved across the bedroom floor and was completely out of reach.

I was still alone, but that would change soon and then, on Monday, I'd rise in the darkness and drive the two and a half hours south to New Haven for another week of exile in the classroom and solitary confinement in my apartment on West Rock Avenue. Trudging up the three front steps outside the house like Willy Loman, and up on to the grey and white porch, I'd press my key into the lock cylinder. Carl, the older German Shepard in the apartment next door, would offer his monotonic bark in welcome.

"Hi, Carl, good boy. Good boy. It's just me," I'd say through the wall. I'd put my bag down and slowly push the door closed behind me. Click.

God, I hated that sound.

Chapter Twenty

The Great Northwest

As 2006 unfolded, I was afraid. I had done some backsliding. Nothing new there. Woulda, coulda, shoulda. Less than a year before, though shocked that we were really and truly headed for demise, I had rebounded quickly and I was beginning to take care of myself properly once again. Acceptance. The truth setting me free. So much of my previous forty years had been based on making accommodations: subjugating for the larger needs of the local community. Mi familia.

I had dusted myself off, though, and was feeling hopeful, but then in the spring, Kate had a mishap and like pulling that barn jacket off the hook in the garage on the first frosty morning in October, I slipped her misfortune around my shoulders and chose the road that was familiar, the road I'd tramped smooth for much longer than the twenty years we'd been together, and said, "I can help."

I did not understand in the moment, but my willingness to subjugate again, to deny my basic need to become whole is what made me feel embarrassed, in a deep place. I had almost broken an essential (and unhealthy) behavior and my retreat to the familiar was fear-based and so, of course, that was nothing to be proud of. I did not realize that I was making a down payment on the ensuing year of emotional pain. In some way, though, that stumble seems to have been almost pre-ordained since the timing led me, ultimately, to Patricia and Vermont.

Kate's skepticism should have been the railroad crossing signal that almost anyone else would have seen and accepted. For me, wobbling on my new training wheels a bit, it offered a challenge—we can make this work again. "I can do this." The rest of that year became one of my biggest ever marketing efforts. I acted my part well, but I had lost my center and I lived almost continually in the future, planning for what might be, instead of engaging directly with what was happening all around me—if I had only taken the initiative to see.

So I overlooked the *Glamour* and *Self* magazines that were scattered around the house when I returned on the weekends during that year. Or Kate's excitement about getting waxed—a Brazilian!—and new, "sassy" haircuts. She had once said to me as we entered a party, years before, that she had no intention of hanging on my arm the whole night since the goal was to "meet new people!" My introversion swooned in eager anticipation at that prospect. And then, with me absent for 70% of the week, each weekend became a repeat of the conversation outside the party that night, as I was introduced to Andrea and Stan and Stephanie and Chas ("He's gay and so cute and the whole thing about getting naked on the couch and watching a movie the other night was just so silly, I mean, there's no *way* anything would have happened!").

In late October, at their mini-farm in Little Compton, Andrea and Stan hosted a Halloween party, on their back acreage, with a small tent and lots of fire pits around the backyard. I wore my Elvis mask and felt that I had really developed my "Priscilla, honey, get me mah valium" and "Thank you very much" lines, which were lost on Kate who kept asking, "Why are you *saying* that?" with some serious eye-rolling. When I looked across the table and saw her standing behind Stan with her tongue down his throat for five seconds that felt like an hour, I went out to our car by way of the bar table, where I grabbed a bottle of Chardonnay that was three quarters full so that I could practice "Thank you very much" without annoying interruptions.

Later, when I was discovered, my inquiry about the table display got only another eye roll and an "Oh for heaven's sake, Shaun. It was just *Stan*." Stan the Man. I yam what I am.

I was profoundly exhausted and very lost. After only six months since I'd convinced myself to try one more time, this visual was a large bucket of ice water smack to the face. I did not make the connection at the time, but the disappointment I felt was similar to the failed boat purchase from Michael. Promises of resurrection in each case had been dashed and it's never any fun to return to the starting blocks.

Kate was on a tear, making new friends. Not many new friends for me, just the stalwarts who always came through.

Andrew and I had worked together in San Francisco. Technically, he had reported to me, and now, as he learned of my situation, he had created a job offer and living situation (with him) in Seattle where, technically, I'd be reporting to him. The head of the private school where I was teaching in New Haven was offended and curt when I resigned just before the March break. Teachers sought out Hopkins School as a career and rejecting their package was an affront, especially since in my position as a technology director I was better compensated than almost anyone on the faculty.

Seattle is where I healed and became whole again.

For the first six months, there was no bed. I jury-rigged an arrangement in the back room that involved a nightly set up and daily break down, but these rituals were therapy and then there was the benefit of those French doors that—starting in April—I was able to keep open until almost Christmas.

Learning to be alone again. Getting to know myself. Accepting the stillness. I used to seek these things out and, like a warrior, protect against those who would invade the quiet. Now, like a victim of a head-on collision, I was learning to walk again and observing what had been offered in trade along the way through agreements forged over twenty years.

Slowly, though, patterns emerged. Every night at just after 4 A.M., a jet liner made a slow half circle arc above the house, headed for SeaTac. FedEx, perhaps. A black cat, making nightly rounds, came by next, shocked to see me (again) on the floor, returning my gaze as dawn tickled the horizon line to the east, trying three or four colors quickly before revealing what was really the master plan.

And in that backyard where I'd helped Andrew build a freestanding deck and patio made of concrete blocks that he said looked "Really boss!" when we were done, there was also an enormous tree that dominated the neighborhood, just on the other side of the fence. I supposed that the tree had few friends and, unlike The Giving Tree, the story read to my kids, where the tree offers more and more and finally offers the ultimate sacrifice to appease an unappreciative partner, this one simply stood—majestic and alone and wise. It was *my* friend though. Only, like so many human encounters, I never got the chance to tell Big Ed why he mattered. Big Ed, that's what I called him. It was in the middle of a long period of insomnia while lying with the French doors open to the back yard that the words escaped me late one night. Just Big Ed. That's all.

A recurring auditory bookmark from that time was the sound of Big Ed's massive leaf structure—in motion always, an ongoing editorial for my benefit alone, it seemed. Sometimes it was like punctuation, sprinkling metronomic counterpoint throughout the internal conversation. Other times—my most cherished—Ed would roar his approval by offering a shudder that ran from the lowest branch on his massive trunk to the very smallest leaf at the pinnacle of two centuries spent stretching toward a point 93 million miles distant. Like a dog on the beach, just after dropping a sopping wet tennis ball.

It was the biggest thing around. From the trail that surrounds Lake Washington, I could see it at a distance from either direction, like a visible magnetic north. And in that way, it offered solace as my daily forays took me farther and farther from home base on long runs. I could always look over my shoulder and there would be Ed, stoic and proud and reassuring.

I hadn't thought about any of these things until years later, on a Thursday when Andrew called for a chat we had put off for too long. "How are things in the neighborhood?" I asked, to reassert the importance my stay had been for me. "Remember that big tree...in the back yard? The guy behind us cut it down." I don't remember the rest of the call. But I do remember lying on the floor next to the open doors in the midst of a three-day run of sleeplessness, amazed that I could squeeze out a few more tears and whispering, "Am I ever going to be okay again?" And Ed shuddered.

Chapter Twenty-One

2015

Patricia had been up for an hour and I could hear quiet music from the room opposite our bedroom, where she was in the midst of her daily yoga practice. It was late January, and with the annual thaw behind us, some light returning at the end of the day, and the Red Sox pitchers reporting to training in just a few weeks, spring was feeling more like a guarantee than a concept.

Lying on my back, with the sloped ceiling an arm's length away, I found myself walking up a ramp in a Northampton parking garage nine years earlier, when I met Patricia for the first time.

I had just flown in from Seattle and she was picking me up for a weekend at her family farm to determine if what we had felt in phone conversations had any potential for the long haul.

I dropped my suitcase when we were close enough for a hug, and after an extended kiss, I looked up to see a couple in a car behind us and two big smiles.

You must remember this: a kiss is still a kiss.

Three nights later, I was back in the kitchen of the house in Seattle, warming up some fettucine alfredo as Andrew asked, "So how did the weekend go?"

"Pretty good, pretty good."

"You and Patricia got along okay?"

"Yeah." And a long pause. Then, "Yeah, it went well. I'm engaged."

Andrew snorted and pushed me away.

"Get the fuck out of here. Oh yeah, I'm sure."

"I'm telling you," I said with a smile.

He stepped back from the stove and cocked his head to the side, much like any Labrador Retriever I'd ever had. He looked me up and down – twice.

"Deane Daddy! For real? Wow. Are you sure about this?"

"I am. I'm sure."

Then we looked down at the sauce that was bubbling slightly as we both shook our heads, slowly.

"Huh." This from Andrew, and since I couldn't come up with a better summary, we left it at that.

I rolled to my left side just as a quick, chilly breeze lifted the window shade by an inch or two and blew a bookmark off the small bookcase onto the small braided scatter rug below. The top of the duvet cover rippled twice and blew some stray hairs back off my forehead. "Skunk was out last night," I observed and maybe I said that aloud, quietly, as I swung back to my right, lifted up the covers, and placed my feet squarely on the complementary rug on my side of the bed.

Recently, I had been leaving my cell phone on the bureau because I had read something about disturbed sleep if the battery in the phone was within five feet of your pillow. Easy enough to address by keeping it out of reach. As I lifted it on this Monday morning, I could see "straight off" (as my old Australian office mate would have said) that I had received a number of voicemails, since the screen was full of notifications. I did not have my glasses nearby, but I could see that most, if not all, of the calls were from "Dad."

"Uh oh." And I did say this out loud, just as Patricia emerged from her small studio room.

"Wassup?" she said with a smile. She looked as though she had been up for hours, not minutes, as I stumbled around in my lingering state of hibernation.

"Dad. Incoming."

"Uh oh," she echoed.

"First tea, then crisis," I said and grabbed the bannister on the left and stepped off onto the first of fourteen polished oak steps down to the first floor.

As the kettle rumbled to life, and with my glasses providing a major assist, I began with the oldest message from 5:24 A.M. Somehow, I had missed all of the calls, but then I could see that I had flipped the ringer off. Good thing we are not going toe to toe with the Russkies, I mulled.

"Shaun. Are you there? Ah *shit!*" That impatience—enough of that for a lifetime, I thought as I lifted the tea bag out of my cup and in one practiced move swung it in a short arc to the compost canister on the counter, whose lid I had removed and positioned as a backboard for the three-point attempt. Nothing but net.

Second message, 5:28 A.M.

"Now look, I need help here, Shaun. Please. Please. Just answer the phone. I really don't know what I'm going to do..."

Instead of finishing that message or trying any of the others, I called directly.

"Dad, what's going on?"

"It's Phyllis, she fell."

"Where?"

"On the stairs and..."

Christ, I thought. So predictable. I had tried to get them to do something about full-time living on their first floor but he tuned that out every time I raised the issue.

"Where is she now?"

"Well, at the bottom of the stairs." It was if he was saying "well, D'UH!"

"Still?" Lord.

"911 is on the way," he started, "but I'm going now, too."

"You're going along with her?"

"No, I am going to the hospital, too. Doctor Warren said I need to go, too. That was one of the messages I left. Didn't you get it?"

"Well, no, I called back instead. I don't understand."

"I fell outside yesterday and hit my head on the concrete steps. When I got myself back inside, I had a blackout for a moment. Doctor Warren wants me to go to the hospital and have them check me out."

"Dad?"

"Shaun, listen to me. Before you come to the hospital, stop at the house and go to my bedroom."

"Okay, what do you need?"

"No, no. Just look around everywhere. Do you understand?"

"No. Look around?"

"Yes," he clipped me off, impatiently. "Just look everywhere, there are secret drawers behind things."

I had no idea what he was talking about until three hours later after I had been in his house for ten minutes and had found the first envelope. That one had $2,200 in twenty-dollar bills, wrapped with a decaying purple rubber band. Ten minutes after that, I had six envelopes next to me on the bed. On the back of each envelope, in pencil, a list of figures with all but the last item crossed out. I felt that I did not need to count every bill in each of the envelopes but if I added up the sums listed, I was in the middle of approximately $17,000, mostly in twenty dollar bills, but there were also occasional fifties and hundreds.

I called Patricia. You'll never guess.

"You'd better look everywhere," she said as we got ready to sign off.

"Care to narrow that down some? He said there were drawers 'behind' and I have no idea what that means," I explained as I pulled out the top drawer in the nightstand next to his bed. As I reached to the back and down behind the bottom drawer, it did feel as though there was some obstruction back there, and once

I had that drawer out, too, I discovered a cache of four more envelopes. Now up to $23,000.

I was getting lightheaded. I found myself in a more defensible position than I had been at the age of ten while rifling through my father's top bureau drawer. Back then, I found a few Trojans wrapped in blue foil and only a vague idea of what they might be used for. This was better than back then, yet I still felt that I was not allowed to be looking and felt furtive as a result.

I went out to the car and emptied the small daypack I had brought along, so that I could get the cash out of the house and to someplace safer. As I pulled out into traffic and headed to the hospital, about twenty minutes later, I called Patricia again.

"Survey says?" I said using my best Richard Dawson inflection.

"Yes?"

"Thirty-two thousand dollars."

"Yikes."

I was halfway to the front door of the hospital when I stopped in mid-step and considered that my Kelty daypack was still in the car. *What are the chances*, I thought? I would be in an entirely indefensible spot if that one random break-in had me shaking my head over spilled milk, so I sauntered back to the car, blowing on my hands to warm them up a bit.

Walking through the lobby of the hospital with the pack slung over my shoulder, it felt transparent. I approached the information desk and the guard seemed to give me a wink and a thumbs up as if to acknowledge, "My man! We see you, looking sharp."

The elders never returned to their home. No scenario arose where they could have lived independently, and though my father talked a good game, he embraced the care that was available to them both and the opportunity to take a break. Thus, it became my opening to start to lobby for a move closer to us, in Vermont.

A cycle of agreement, resistance, and acceptance played a few times through, including once when plans were all set for the move and I went to pick them up for the three-hour drive, only to be told by my father that they decided that they were not going after all. I did not see it as "luck" at the time, but the fact that the pipes in their house had burst and that the sunroom and much of the downstairs had flooded during their stay at the Southeast Rehabilitation Center meant that there was no viable living situation to return to and so the deal was sealed.

Months later, I was back in his bedroom again, deerstalker on and magnifying glass at the ready. We did, in fact, find even more cash in envelopes that I was sure I had looked in on the fly, but the fact was that I almost put $11,000 in twenty-dollar bills into the dumpster out in the driveway.

During these revisits, I began to find memorabilia of all sorts and it began to blow the mist away from some low-lying areas that had always been unclear to me and that I was even completely unaware of. It was a strange experience: the sort of thing that one does after parents have died. Yet mine were still here and accessible. Events might be corroborated, if I could find a way to weave in any discoveries to a conversation about Depends or the resident cat's eating habits.

Underneath the bed and in some of the lower bureau drawers were caches of correspondence that in many cases included both sides of a running conversation—between my father and my mother, or with Phyllis, after they had met. Many pieces were in the original envelopes and so date-marked. The timestamps enabled me to focus a spotlight on a crucial time period during which I had never felt that I was in the loop, while my adolescent hormones and political events raged. In a very literal sense, I was able to lay out a chronology on the bed, starting in about 1967.

On the outside of an envelope from that same year, a notation of *"Proof that Betty forged my signature and fraudulently cashed my war bonds."* The underbelly of my parents's marriage and dissolution was on full display and I did not feel the need to continue down those tracks—maybe later. Some other time.

In an olive-green metal container about the size of a shoebox, there was another set of letters. The box may have been used to carry ammunition in the war and had clasps at each end to hold the lid in place. It looked like something that could have been picked up at the Great Eastern Corporation or the Army-Navy store in Cambridge—two places I visited often at about the time that all of these letters had been written.

Mixed in with the letters were some photographs—mostly wallet-sized and with the feel of the Purdy Studio shots we got for our high school yearbooks. In this case, they were all of Judy Rubin, who was now, obviously, a central player in the post-Betty, pre-Phyllis period. And though my mother correctly claimed to have told us that he would not be back, it was the "why" part of her assertion that I'd never been able to resolve. The photographs of Judy were familiar and I knew that I had met her but not how or where.

Back in Vermont, a week or two later, during an evening when Patricia was teaching yoga, I carried a perspiring bottle of Pinot Grigio and one long stemmed wineglass—a wedding present from my mother's older sister—out to the screened-in porch. From her position atop two overstuffed pillows in front of the porch door, Riley huffed twice to let me know that there was woodchuck ambling toward the forsythia bush. "Good girl, thank you," I said as I sat down in the brown wicker chair to become acquainted with Judy and, in ways unexpected, with my Dad.

Chapter Twenty-Two

Judy

Before I had even crossed one leg over the other or taken a first sip of the amber hued wine, I went out to the flatbed trailer in the garage, where clutter from my father's house sat, ready for review and dispensation. There were boxes with scrapbooks and mementos of a journey through nine or ten different decades, but I was focused on one box of documentation from the late sixties when my father taught at Bentley College in Waltham.

He had started a theatre group called "The Experimental Theatre" that started out with readings: *Spoon River Anthology*, *Letters of an Irish Parish Priest*—things like that. Quickly, though, the troupe had moved on to full scale productions of *Lion in Winter*, *The Caine Mutiny*, and *Moby-Dick*. In a folder of publicity shots, I found one 8x10 glossy taken of the entire group during the production of *Moby-Dick*, all on stage and beaming.

Front and center was my father wearing what my brother and I called his mad scientist glasses—frames that were artifacts from the 1950s that gave him a slightly crazed look when he smiled big as he was doing in this photograph. I was reminded of an image I had downloaded from the internet recently that was a stylized graphic of a guy from the post-Sputnik period, wearing a Trilby hat and holding a martini glass over a sentence in an 18-point font that proclaimed, "Great News! I'm high as fuck!"

To my father's right and slightly forward of the group was Judy in an A-line jumper that ended two inches above her knees.

That in itself was not remarkable, but I was reminded that in 1968 it might have been considered a "mini," and she had the legs to pull it off. When the shutter leaves opened for just 1/125th of a second on that day west of Boston, there was no way to know that fifty years worth of thirty-one million seconds per year would elapse before I was standing in that very spot, temporarily divorced from my Pinot Grigio and watching a few more of the jigsaw pieces slipping home as a John Prine lyric played from some cranial file drawer: "Now, don't you know all he saw was all there was to see."

I did remember her now, more in context, but just as a visual. Perhaps we met only at this performance before I drove Sheila home and lost my virginity around the corner from her house, in the back seat of my mother's red Rambler American. The appeal was clear: she was petite and therefore complemented my dad's height. She had a big smile and her blonde hair, parted simply on one side, fell to her shoulders and up in a simple flip that made it easy to imagine her as a cheerleader—which is how she had started out a dozen years and two kids earlier. *Dad needed a cheerleader*, I thought, during the time when he upended all that was stable, while Chris and I rode the end of the whip, as the snake whirled across our frozen pond of an early winter.

I sauntered back to the porch and pulled the sliding door open a few inches for some air, then sat back and removed the lid from the government issued ammo container and grabbed the packet of letters and cards that were wrapped with a purple rubber band.

May 12, 1967

Dear Mr. Deane,

Thank you for being a fine teacher and a unique human being. It is impossible for me to express adequately the gratitude I feel for your interest in me and your efforts in my behalf. Possessing no definite goal before entering your class three years ago, I am now aware of the direction of my life. Not only was I unaware of my future, but I also lacked a personal philosophy. Under three years of your guidance, I have grown more in intellect and spirit than in the previous twenty-four years. Your training in English Composition taught me how to write and that accomplishment amazes me. Furthermore, through each successive paper I unearthed thoughts and feelings that shook the foundations of my life. Since then I have been gradually discovering who and what I am—and it is not easy. In retrospect, it is quite clear to me that this was precisely your intent. I am as responsible as you are for my acquiring confidence and personal ability. You have laid out the course and I am running it, with miles to go.

Concerning our relationship in the past year, I regard you as one of those few friends.

Sincerely,

Judy Rubin

P.S. A subtle suggestion concerning your reply containing directions to your home—please answer either in Sanskrit or type, not in your inimitable longhand, because I do not wish to end up in Utica.

Smiling, I looked up just as a doe and two of her babies (twins?) crossed tentatively in front of the woodshed, headed for the stream beyond the rock wall in our backyard.

So yes, it was 1967 then—and everything was new—for all of us. As I began the journey through this secret but not so secret packet of correspondence, I was enjoying my time with Judy and I could understand the draw. It's artificial to some extent, since in letters (and love letters, especially) one's best foot is undeniably out front, but I could see qualities that were not part of the marriage or family that I was a participant in. In ours, teasing and joking had a bite and a goal. At the same time, I was seeing Dad through a filter that I would never have been able to access otherwise. The lover. The schmoozer. As I read more, the short poem by Mary Howitt came to mind—"The Spider and the Fly"—and I was not sure why, so soon, there was any sense of portent.

May 30, 1967

Dear Judy,

So all right, already, it's typed! Not only that, but a map is enclosed: despite the insult to my handwriting, the invitation still stands. Is the 24th still good for you, about 7:00? If not, no problem in changing. There's also a self-interpreting test enclosed, which you might find interesting. I ran across it in college and have periodically re-taken it to watch for any changes. It correlates well, and answers to particular questions are sometimes more revealing than the final results.

Thank you for your letter, which isn't superfluous at all. MY efforts in your behalf are negligible and you're entitled to them. My interest is partially selfish, because you have given me at least as much as you suggest I have given you. My kind of teaching is produced by having great people to talk to and at. The diffidence you once expressed in the 1890's course about your abilities in relation to others in the course was misplaced. You are the best I have ever taught, and so far as I can see your limits have not even been set. Knowing such a person is present,

I am inclined to do more and say more of what I believe than I otherwise would, just as I suspect that you write in papers what can't otherwise be easily said. Ironically, you know me better than people I have known for much longer; probably you wish you didn't! Anyway, despite what I said at the last meeting about men and women not being allowed to be friends, I hope the fact of the end of the course won't prove me right.

Sincerely,

Paul Deane

P.S. Classes are over, so for God's sake use my first name and forget the titles—okay?

The charm machine was on and turned up high. I did not understand about "the test." I did find a few psychological profile tests in the boxes of papers and books we had pulled from the house. I was inclined to believe that it was probably an early version of the Myers-Briggs tests I've taken a number of times in the workplace. "Collaboration is the new paradigm! Pivot your skills for success in the workplace of 2020. Understand how your weaknesses can be strengths and how to use them most effectively!"

June 6, 1967

Dear Mr. Deane,

Thank you for your letter. After I wrote to you, I looked over some of my papers with your written comments on them and decided that your handwriting is not as bad as I thought. It's worse! I took that test you sent and here are the results: Aesthetic—39, Religious—38, Political—36,

Theoretical—32, Social—24, and Economic—11. The 24th of June is fine.

Some of those poems by Stephen Crane are shattering, particularly, "War is Kind." A strange and most frightening thing happened to me after I read it, something that has happened only once before. That was when I finished The Last of the Just, by Andre Schwrtz-Bart. I cried and couldn't stop. I've never felt so sad in my life as I did on those two occasions. Perhaps I identify too strongly with their suffering, but I don't think so because I haven't suffered such terrible things. When I read those things, I felt as if I were standing there in the reality of the horror, and a great wave of compassion swept over me and this emotion was overwhelming. How can suffering ennoble one? Often I feel as if I am in a remote place looking down at humanity and feeling so much.

I am looking forward to meeting your wife and having dinner with you both.

Sincerely,

Judy Rubin

Meeting your wife? What the hell? Just outside the slider door, a ruckus erupted: a small bluebird and a brilliant red cardinal with a very dark back were posturing over the left side of the feeder, even though there was enough room for a half dozen of their buddies on the bottom tray. The cardinal deferred and the blue bird looked my way as I offered a thumbs up, which seemed to do the trick as she was immediately back on task.

The wine glass was sweating profusely now and I thought, as I took another sip, that the dew point must be on the rise. *Boy, that's got a nice snap,* I thought, *I'll have to get another bottle on my next trip downtown.*

Now that I had considered the most recent letter more

carefully, it struck me that Judy had been trying to clarify the intent of the invitation and to her credit, she was making no assumptions. *That's deft*, I thought and nodded my head in her direction. Another thumbs up.

Thursday

My dearest everything

Your poetry collection is marvelous. Forgive my not reacting more warmly before class, but I always have to look at something carefully before the impact of it hits me. You have unerring good taste; your choices are unimprovable -- and interesting! I read all the poems over breakfast and it was a rough meal because the poems hit very hard and you have arranged them climactically so that the impact just keeps building.

> My own heart's lady, with no gainsaying
> You shall be always wholly till I die,
> In all my fight against every bitter thing.
> The voice of reason bids that I put love by
> But love more faithfully.
> This is the end for which we two are met.

When I first read the poem twelve years ago, I didn't know that you existed. You were seventeen and just about to be married probably; I had been married for six years. I lived in a bad house, I had been fired by B.U., I could see little in the future. The first two lines were the most beautiful I had ever read. I thought, give me a love that is worth dying for, or better yet, worth living for... I knew I *didn't have it and had never had it. My marriage had never exalted me; I couldn't see that it ever would. I said, sometime I will be able to say these lines to someone who already exists, who will like them and feel my feelings when I say them. I love you. If your name were not printed here and there in the poetry collection, I still would know who had put it together. I know your tastes and the guts that would assemble just these works and no others.*

Some of the letters were short. These tended to be from Judy and were perhaps two or three paragraphs beneath the "JSR" monogram in two-inch high green letters at the top of the page. Most were not dated, and I had to make some editorial guesses to place these in the timeline where they seemed most appropriate. As I read through this next one, inexplicably, a short line from Norman Maclean's book that I had used in a friend's eulogy came to the forefront:

"On some of the rocks are timeless raindrops. Under the rocks are the words, and some of the words are theirs."

Dear Paul,

I want to write a beautiful, memorable letter to you, one that someone could discover a hundred years from now and feel my love and understand and be filled with awe. But I am not going to. I shall sit here and hold your hand and give you what is most dear to me so I can become complete.

Once I told you that I was waiting for something. It was you. I have much to say and I know you do too. If we think of doing this in terms of weeks, it seems futile. Think of the years. I love you.

Judy

As I pulled another puzzle piece from something less than the hundred years she imagined, I nodded again to honor her hope that someone would feel and understand. Patricia had pulled into the driveway and I could hear her with the groceries as she entered the kitchen and greeted Riley.

The sun was about to drop below the tree line beyond Rob's house, but for the moment, a few stray beams worked their way through the rear of the wood shed, highlighting pieces of dry and blonde colored birch. I knew that the trajectory of the remaining letters would not be uplifting, but for that moment, it was important to honor that purity and the time when a heart finds a match.

Now the bluebird was back, accompanied by its mate. Riley had joined me and was pushing a headless stuffed duck into my left leg to announce that our pack was now reunited. I stood up slowly to close the slider, trying not to disturb the blue couple. As I placed the letters back in the long metal box, I said to Riley, "More later," and she cocked her head to the right.

* * *

On Monday evenings, Patricia teaches yoga. The clocks had been moved ahead the day before so that the sun was a bit higher and the colors in the backyard were more saturated. As a temporary bachelor, I was stationed back in the sunroom, to continue my voyeurism, with a box in my hand that housed letters from almost half a century before. Excitement hung in the room as I approached the task again.

All I had done to that point was to arrange the pieces of correspondence chronologically, according to the postmarks on the envelopes. A number of them had no date, or no postmark, but almost all of them had stamps. What did that imply? Delivered by hand? Held back until the time seemed right—or better?

The sequence was not a perfect call and response, but there was enough continuity that I had to assume that all of them were, in fact, received. Although I was making my way through the pile for the first time, it felt as though I could be plotting the arc of the relationship on graph paper, especially since I was beginning to experience some foreshadowing within the letters here and there, but I was also acutely aware of, and confused by, the underlying timeline that I had actually lived through.

Their first exchange was in 1967 and during the time when my parents were headed toward divorce. Chicken and egg? Although I had only read the first few letters, I knew that dissolution was on the horizon, since I had attended the wedding of my father and Phyllis in December 1970. Holding these bookends in my memory added an element of suspense to the exercise. If I had stumbled upon these letters without knowing the players, it would have been easy to assess them quickly as "sad" or to brush them off perhaps as "shit happens."

As I followed the lobs and volleys back and forth, the emotions were unusual. On one hand, I was meeting—and enjoying—Judy for the first time. Conversely, I was offered a view—angles—of my father that I had not been privy to and, naturally, I was looking for opportunities to corroborate my own world-view and belief system. I knew that it was next to impossible to remain objective and tried to keep that notion present as I delved deeper into the box and the past.

> Paul, I love you. I am sitting here loving you and me together and crying and writing God-awful reams of hopeless poetry. Beware not. This isn't a psychotic letter. It's one full of heart's pain. I love you and I miss you and God I feel so empty and broken and oh shit, this is a psychotic letter.
>
> I know you love me. Please don't think I feel deserted. I don't, but what I do feel is aimlessness. Not knowing what is going to happen is shattering because for the past few months I had been so sure. I love you. Yes, this is a nutty letter. All I am thinking of is your phone call tomorrow morning. Will you take me to lunch someday again? That

was fun, huh? In fact, everything was fun with you. That was me, you know, all the time. Don't worry, I would never do anything to myself. Sometimes I feel I want to, but it's too god damned easy. I love you, you know. I give you my life, dear Paul. I want to cry out to you so many things and I must not. Please find your way to one or the other of us before we all perish.

Yours always,

Judy

February, 1968

The whole world seems bent on telling you what's wrong with you (which is probably proof that you're better than they are and they know it); I'm telling you what's right with you, and my judgment is better than all of theirs.

Nobody is more worthy than you of respect and admiration. Your presence on this earth is a demand and a fulfillment, as though evolution had been forcing in this one direction to this time, to you. Certainly all our lives, all the separate, several parts have conspired to add you to me and me to you. The wonder is that the two halves of the perfect whole did not meet and fitted together—without a seam. Lovers do become each other, yet remain separate: completed and incomplete without each other.

I knew always, I think, that you were there, waiting for me to find you. I wanted to be ready for that time. Some instinct kept telling me,

"Be ready for her when she comes. She will want what you are. It is for this she that you are what you wanted to be.

So far as your parents and friends and town are concerned, you are now more mine than theirs. Close your ears to them. They want you to be like them, to settle for an average bigoted mediocrity, to wear your hair at a "prescribed" length and fashion, to lengthen your skirts, to live the "normal" life of acceptance and self-betrayal. You're a colossus in that town, a giant of honesty and ability. You took what happened to you in high school and instead of running away and knuckling down, you stayed and shoved it right in their faces; they don't forgive that kind of strength. You decided on becoming educated and you began to get it—yourself. You decided on your personality. You showed professional trained teachers that you were not their peer but their superior.

I can pay you no higher compliment than to say that I choose to love you because I know you; I do not want any change or "improvement"; I demand that you do not change, in fact. Do what you have to do, what you want to do. There is no way in which you could be superior to what you are now, in my estimation. And no one, not parents, family, friends or associates, knows you better than I do. They are not satisfied with you because they don't understand you. I do. I am.

The difference in tone was striking, even though I had only made my way through a small percentage of the complete package.

I was still getting to know Judy. She was entirely different from the other women in my father's life—my mom and, eventually, Phyllis—playful and obviously vulnerable.

Still attempting to maintain an open ear, the replies from him at times were reading like a set of lecture notes. I had the feeling that when he sat down to write the most recent one, he was thinking more about the construction of a convincing argument and grammatical hijinks rather than spilling his guts. Every once in a while, there was a real "zinger" that stopped me cold and caused me to consider implications of what had come before he ever pressed pen to paper (and what was on the horizon.)

"*So far as your parents and friends and town are concerned, you are now more mine than theirs*." It would take a lot of therapy sessions to understand how that approach had affected my upbringing, but the notion of ownership, domination, and pulling back from the real world—us against them—was an absolute during the decades after Chris died and throughout my father's relationship with Phyllis. Now comes a subtle urgency. The wild abandon of the early days was being replaced by more explanation, an occasional apology, glances to the rearview, and exhortations to persevere.

Feb 29, 1968

Paul,

I love you and I do not say how much because I cannot. I just love you so. I was awful tonight. I am sorry. We have fewer and fewer chances to be together and I refused to discuss us tonight and just thought of myself. I am so sorry. I love you and could sense your need to be close to me and I feel as though I shut you off. I'll never do it again. I could never hurt you and I fear that I did. You are the finest person I have ever known and I feel so secure in your loving me and your being all mine. You are perfection to me and what you said of being in awe of me is also what I feel for you. When will we be together forever? It will be a unique union, my dearest man. And it's 2 o'clock in the morning so good night my dearest, sweetest love. I'll dream of you.

Your woman,

Judy

September, 1968

Dearest,

I can't fully realize that a year has gone since last September first, because that night is as clear in my mind as though it were yesterday. You were just sitting across from me last night, it seems, and words have been spoken that were not imagined or expected—words still amazing. It seems you have just said you can't believe that I could love you. Yet a year later those feelings and the words are still the same. They are said to and felt for a person I know much better and much differently, but they are the same. There were fewer fears a year ago, just the joy of realization of each other.

I still want for you what you have never had enough of and consequently find it hard to accept what you said a month ago when you called me in Hingham—that you realized no one in the world cared what happened to you but me. I hope that isn't true, there should be many.

We've developed a whole vocabulary of words

together, terms you said Monday night that you are sick of hearing. I know what you mean. Let's use them no more. Let's think of the bright warm days of autumn, which I smell in the air again, the exhilaration we both felt in each other and that I, at least, still feel.

The year has attuned my whole body and mind to you. I can never again not be a part of you. I must express it in words so brief and familiar—I love you, Judy. All of what I am is in those words.

Paul

When I returned to New England from Seattle to be with Patricia and to live in Southern Vermont, an ad on the bulletin board of the local food cooperative got my attention. "Be a Radio Show Host!" The local, low-power community station had openings for DJs—experienced or not—and soon I was pushing electrons down the wire on Sunday evenings. My musical library expanded exponentially, and during times of reflection or self-absorption, I often had a background soundtrack running that added some zest to the tasks at hand or sometimes offered an insight or two.

As I pulled the next group of dense, single-spaced (typed) pages from the shoebox, an obscure song by Peter Wolf and Neko Case celebrated the green fields of summer and the encouragement to lie down together. This next batch had no envelopes. None of them included dates, but in an obvious way, even reading just the first paragraph or two, they were stationed between the beginning and the end.

Dearest Judy:

I'm writing instead of talking because I want you to know that some thought has gone into it. As usual -- no irony or sarcasm meant —you are right and I am wrong. We always talk about your insecurities and hang-ups; we don't talk about mine except in big, general terms. Maybe they're the same things. I too am drawn back to my former life; I too miss parts of it desperately. I say very little about it because you invariably say, "Go back to her." That isn't the point but still you say it and I shut up. I know what it feels to you to have given up so much and to be still in the home where it used to be. I realize that I am not enough ever to compensate for it. You wish that we had never happened and that you had never committed yourself to me to this extent. I am a constant reminder. And you are to me. So I look for flaws, for reasons why you aren't good enough, for reasons to reject you just as you do about me.

I see that you aren't a good housekeeper, though you iron and wash and sweep; I see that you're very badly organized and I have always been a methodical person. I see that you turn against your own best interests and that you will let no one really advise you. And I look for more and more: every raised eyebrow I see as a portent of danger, and so I cause the danger to be sure it happens. It's paranoia, isn't it? I'm the sick one, along with you, just in a different way. I see actions that you do as cold, colder than Betty's. Perhaps they aren't. We have difficulty accepting each other as we are, though we loved each other in the beginning because of what we are. I have felt it as all hypocrisy on your part -- that now you want to change all the things that attracted you to me in the beginning. Yet I'm doing the same thing.

You say that I'm complicated and that you don't understand me; I feel the same. I'm always demanding that you change, but I do precious little changing. And I think it's a matter of degree: I've given up more than you have; I don't have my home or children or normal life in any sense. I have only you: so I ask impossible things from you that make up for what I've lost, for impossible proof that it was worth giving it all up for. Your insecurities are not quite the same, though they do involve losses and the same deep ones. You have the financial problem -- as I do too -- along with the others, and you have this terrible sense of failure as a person—wife, mother, daughter, mistress, and all the rest. So you pick at me: you allow the fights to go on because they prove that I'm a bastard but also truths come out of them and prove to you that you're a flop also. The fights convince you that you've made a mistake in loving me and breaking up your home, and they show me that you are a poor reason for doing the same.

What I want of course is to be married to you, to take you out of this place full of memories to another nice house in another nice place and to start as you and me. The irony is that I was never an impossible demander with Betty and from what you say directly and indirectly, you asked for very little from Roger. Yet from each other we ask the impossible. Because, as you said of Diane and Larry, we can get out of it, we can stop the relationship and we know it and so we have nothing here to even hang on to. If we were married, we wouldn't fight about these things because in marriage we would have the very securities we have now lost and are afraid the other person cannot supply.

That is why it was important for me to be here this week and fix things in your house, like cabinets, etc., to show you that there is someone who will do these small, normal things for you that you can't or shouldn't have to do yourself. They are just a way of my saying I want to take care of the TV repairman for you and call plumbers and worry about fuses and balance the checkbook, so your jobs can be the ones you like: because I am sure that you are a good housekeeper and cook and carer for people -- if you had the time, the back-up, if you had a person to take the other things off you. I never wanted to bother with any of these things before, but for some reason, I do with you. For want of a better way of saying it, I want to make your life easier than it has been, to take away the nervousness which is accentuated by your not having time for anything. OK, so this is not apology, promise or anything like these. It's another kind of love letter.

JSR

It is 1:30 A.M. so you can perceive my state of mind. It has occurred to me at this late hour how marvelous and rare it is you found me. The me no one knows. Incredible. Never will it happen to me again. And I know I have discovered the you beneath husband, father and professor. Such a communion of souls exists between us. You know, all one needs in life is for one person, opposite sex of course, who one adores, admires, respects, cherishes, appreciates, and loves and needs for her continuing and breathing in this life, is for that person to know and feel all the emotion you harbor for him. What I mean is what we need is for me to respond to your unutterable worth as a man and a human being and for you to respond to me as a woman who is extremely worthwhile in this life.

If you decide that your life at home is necessary to the three lives entwined there, I shall accept it as I have accepted your return to it. I shall understand and I am not spouting a cliché. What you do I accept because you do it.

Eternal love and everything,

Judy

Monday

Dear Judy,

Maybe this is an unnecessary letter, because a lot of what will be in it we both already know. You said Saturday evening that when you sent me away a week ago, you felt we were through. I did too. You also said that at the time, you didn't care. I did. But I used the idea of a cooling off period as I had the first of August, to think and to evaluate. Both times you came after me not because of serious thinking you had done but because of things that happened to you. The first time Roger and Anna had both clearly rejected you and this time because the children had been badly treated by their father. I feel that you called me because you realized your children were suffering—they needed a father (you asked me Saturday to love you all), and also because of insecurity and loneliness.

Since the first of August, I have tried to face seriously the issues. I don't think you have. I'm not sure that I want to marry you. I'm not sure that I don't. But the point is that I'm looking at you and me, not at children, money, family.

After you had had enough sex, you said to me, "You'd like some more, wouldn't you? Well, you can't have it because it's too late." Granted, you changed your mind, but it was too late, however and I knew you were conceding. That ruined it for me. For about an hour at dinner, you acted the little girl sister, begging for your big sister's attention and approval, a sister a half hour later you claimed to hate. I don't see one shred of evidence that you ever mean to do anything else. Maybe you can't. You say my demands are too huge. All right then, what are they?

Certainly not as you feel, exclusive attention. But I do want to feel important to you and me—I do want open affection, which I didn't have in my marriage. You've known this from the beginning a year ago. I want the knowledge that you are concerned enough about us to be considerate and to think beforehand about the effect of certain words and actions. It isn't any good to apologize after the harm has been done.

You see, I feel that once married to me you will relax immediately back into former habits—one example: you get up and get Owen's breakfast before he leaves for school. But you get up at 8:20 when I'm there and I get my own, which I did for 17 years, and ate it alone, as I did for 17 years. You claimed that this isn't how it would be. I think you will want to have the same freedom to go out at night, to stay up late watching TV and letting me go to bed alone. You told me not that long ago that when you married again you wanted just what you had before only with a new person. So I repeat, I don't see a shred of evidence that you want a better or even different life.

I feel I am being offered a great deal less than I had before, that I'm going to have to fight and struggle for everything that I get, every crumb of appreciation, etc. I feel that you allow things to accumulate—money worries, child worries, school worries—so that the pile becomes so big that you can't face or handle any part of it and therefore you can avoid me. But the most important thing in the world to me and I think it could be to you, is whether you and I marry. Every other issue all summer should have been put to the side.

This is why I'm not sure that I want to marry you. Convince me. I don't see my needs as "demands" or all that excessive or extraordinary. All Saturday evening it was your sister's and brother-in-law's approval you were craving for. Where was I? When did you seek mine? That is the only approval that right now should be of importance to you because everyone else close to you has rejected you.

I can't take a chance with my life that you want anything else. I don't think you are sick, I just think you are lazy and thoughtless about the feelings of people who care for you. You take them for granted and feel you have to do nothing. Well you do. You have to be active and willing and thoughtful about the person who has "given you your life."

I don't honestly and fully know what I want from you. I just don't feel I have you, except for intervals. I need to feel I have you all the time -- not 24 hours a day, not just that you are there for me—not only for you and a few others. I feel I come last. I want to come first—not only, just first. There's room for a lot of others.

I was unaware that it had begun to rain. It was windy, too. The rain was driving to the east and spattered the tall floor-to-roof windows on my right. The door was still open halfway and Riley had her nose pressed against the screen and was snorting in great gulps of humid air. It had become very dark and suddenly a one-two punch of lightning and thunder lifted me off the cushions a bit and pushed some adrenaline through my gut. Patricia's family had a dog that would hide in the closet an hour or two before a storm arrived. Riley continued her rotary breathing, unfazed.

All that remained in the box beside me were letters from Judy. They continued in longhand but were no longer on the same "JSR" stationery. Like the energy of the white-hot relationship, I suppose they had been used up. Sitting alone in an early evening downpour, I had an overwhelming feeling of regret. I was pulling for Judy—more so perhaps than I had for my own mother—but I also understood that there was something stripped down and available to me that one can never have or see in your direct family. Here, I could see the zenith of a relationship born from need, and that flirted with fulfillment, only to hit some Icarian turbulence over the Aegean Sea before the fall.

As I thought back to Betty, to Chris and Judy, and forward to Phyllis, my bleak assessment was that no one gets what they need. Chris just never caught a break. Mom was too tough for her own preservation. Judy got things going too soon, before she had figured herself out, and then circumstance took over and it was wham bam, thank you ma'am.

I was thinking back to the times I babysat my brother, when my parents went out to a movie, or a party, and within the first hour, we'd be in a scrum on the braided rug in the living room as he gave in to my headlock. He always had a buzz cut in these memories and the sensation of his hair on my forearm lingers, five or six decades later. He'd cry from frustration and I'd have to spend the next hour or so convincing him not to tell our parents, which sometimes included bribes or cash for concessions offered.

I stood, stretched, and headed to the kitchen for a second glass of Zinfandel, and as I filled the cobalt blue wine glass, I could barely see the rim through the tears that had welled up in my eyes.

"Ah, shit," I said and wiped them on my right sleeve as I pivoted back toward the sunroom.

Riley was on the porch and sitting in front of my chair. She stared at me as I sat down and continued to do so after I'd positioned myself and picked up the shoebox once again.

"I'm okay," I reassured her, and with that confirmation, she circled three times in her bed and lay down with a sigh.

All that was left now were two letters and a few small cards—all from Judy. Dad had gone dark. It was impossible for me to identify when this next group had been written. No date and no reference to anything in the larger world, but I knew, without considering it for too long, that it had to have been 1969—probably early on. He married Phyllis at the tail end of 1970 and, allowing for a brief courtship, that knocked 1970 out of contention.

I never could understand how he'd been able to become so absent at that time in my life (and my brother's). It always seemed as though a light switch had simply been flicked off. Poof. Now, though, as a light breeze lifted the corner of a tee shirt on the drying rack next to me, it was clear to see that the crescendo that was supposed to have been the answer to his first marriage had sounded and then, in denouement, he had only enough attention to white knuckle the plane into the hillside.

My friend John has offered sage advice on occasion: "Every once in a while, a blind squirrel finds an acorn." Now I understood just one iota more. Now I could see the canvas upon which all of these players circled one another, mostly without contact. In 1969, my unconscious outcries, manifested in multiple arrests for petty offenses and bad acid trips, got no reaction and it confused me. To be ignored is to not matter. Now I could see the distraction inherent in the rest of the family and it provided some clarity, a half century later. More than anything else, I could see and was proud of a thin golden thread of self-reliance that had been pulling me forward, protectively, deftly avoiding the craters and crevasses in the moonscape around me.

Paul,

This is the last communication I shall ever have with you. When we were lovers and friends, you said more than once that if we were ever parted and I was in trouble, no matter your or my circumstances, you would help me. I said the same. I was in trouble Tuesday night. You did not help me. Because Phyllis didn't want you to is no excuse. Being your wife, she should feel no threat from me.

It amazes me that you were puzzled when I would not marry you. Down inside you knew. I never said it, but now

I will. You are a gutless man. You live out a life of fantasy on the stage by playing masculine parts like Ahab and the hero of La Mancha. You spout strength and courage in class as a cover for your cowardice. All you wanted from me was a beautiful woman to dominate. If you could, all your associates would think you were quite a man. You wanted me on display as a token of your manliness. You are not a man. You are a fraud. If I die, even by my own hand, I will be stronger in death than you ever were in life.

Judy

Paul,

My love forever, but too late, I know why I can't teach anymore. The spirit is gone. All our knowledge of what we are together is out now so don't be ready with explanations for the end. I know them, so do you. But they are not important anymore, but it's too late. It's too late, late, late for me. Always has been. There will never be another you ever. And I am not scared or afraid. I am terrified. But you know that. You didn't call me back on Wednesday and I know why. But when you receive this, please call me for the last time. I will try to go to work for the 2 1/2 days school is in session next week. I'll try because I have to tie up loose ends. But I'll be looking for a reason to stay. With you in my life, it was so easy; now it's impossible because of the way I teach. You want me to get in there and give 'em hell, right? Well the body is willing but the spirit isn't.

You know what? I'm not pretty anymore. Strange.

In losing you, I lost myself, my life. Never will I get it again. It's gone. For me, you were infinite in my life. I was so shallow. I did not see what was happening to my one true love in the world. Says a lot for me, doesn't it.

Contrary to what people say, one does not pick up the pieces and go on. Pieces remain pieces. And what we had was so good, magnificent, it was a monument to love, at times, and now real pieces are all around me. Where are our love letters. Did you destroy them?

I made out my will last week and sent it to my lawyer (how mundane) and I left you something I didn't know I possessed until you loved me -- my soul. You will take care of it, I know. Just tuck it inside your own and won't God be pleased?

I want to fall asleep in your arms. I want to fall asleep in your arms.

Goodnight, dear. I love you. I am truly sorry I did not see your needs and your sorrow. Forgive me.

Please call me once more. At night. After the letter. I'll be waiting. The last time; the last call. I love you, Paul, forever. I won't cry. But I'm not pretty anymore.

Judy

*****

and she fell to the beach
like a gull feather
softly into the white sand
the harsh lemon sun
does not warm her
she does not feel the
foamy whiteness of the tide
playing idly at her naked feet
that he had kissed
the sandwind rustles her hair
but she does not know

she knows only
the emptiness and tears
that her lover her life
has left with his
parting
and she lies alone on a
beach
that is as insignificant
to her
as she is now
to him

*****

Lost as a child
bitter as a hag
a bird of scarlet plumage
with broken wings
a loser

And so it was done. Just three cards left, all small, and all postmarked in 1971—the newlyweds' first year. Of course, the tonality was very different. The first two, an obvious attempt to maintain a connection based on the original premise of the lovers' connection, and the last, oddly, an "unethical" request to use words previously published. That in itself was very strange, since one of the items of family lore was my father's self-described abhorrence of plagiarism.

According to him, he included a recitation of a Massachusetts statute against theft in all of his first day classes and a description of how that covered plagiarism and the potential for up to six months in jail. It's a good thing that he retired before Google became ubiquitous.

April 1, 1970

Paul,

Emergency! Please write and tell me the significance of the Christ motif in Moby Dick—I think I know, but I need your help. Time is too short to write down all my ideas now. The teaching of the novel is going beautifully—so if you help me, I'll be grateful.

Thanks,
Sincerely,

Judy

Perhaps you'd rather call.

April 30, 1971

Dear Paul,

Pardon the weird stationery, but I bought it from my Junior Class and I figured I must use it if only to get rid of it. Do you remember that lifeboat problem you gave me 2 years ago? The one about who to throw out? Well, I lost it. Could you please send it to me? I need it desperately. Also, are you teaching any courses that I could "take" at Bentley this summer? No job next year unless I come up with 26 credits by next August.

Roger has lost total interest in the kids. It seems they dirty his carpets when they go there. Can you imagine?

How did the play go? I was thinking of you all weekend, hoping it was a success. I am teaching The Red Badge. Wrote a 22 page beautiful lecture on it. Wish you could see it and pat me on the back!

Judy

November 2, 1971

Dear Paul,

I hope you are well. Thank you for the card in August. I suppose you had a great time away from it all. The boys are fine. Owen is straight A material this year finally. Hope your boys are OK. Chris must be a Junior now. I am taking Geology and Shakespeare this term with a directed readings course for Blinderman, the ass. My God, he's a fool. Anyway, I am writing about that course because the readings are in Jack London. I have read everything, and I plan to use your paper for the basis of mine. As when anyone embarks on something unethical as this, pangs of guilt accompany the action. Also, I am concerned about Blinderman's possible knowledge of your paper's existence. Does he know of it? Was it ever published? My action would not be necessary except for the fact that I must graduate in May or no job! I am taking three mini course and then three more in the Spring. I know you understand all this but understanding doesn't excuse it. It really is hard for me to justify my doing it at all on ethical grounds. I rationalize all the time saying that a damn piece of paper is determining my life and has been for twelve years and I am sick of the whole thing, school. Well, anyway, could you answer my question?

I hope this letter finds you well and content.

Judy

The rain had ceased, and with just twenty minutes or so before the long duvet of darkness that covered New Hampshire was to be pulled across the Green Mountains of Vermont, I sat once again in the gloaming. In the stillness, there were only a few sweet sounds: the cascade of raindrops from the canopy of the maple tree across the driveway to its bottommost leaves, along with a chorus of peepers from the pond at the bottom of our open field.

An exuberant chickadee called to the two of us from the hydrangea bush just outside the sliding door, proclaiming to all that she was still willing to party on, if only for more light.

As I lowered the shoebox, I was surprised at the connection I felt to Judy throughout this process of discovery. A lost soul. Another Chris. By now, I felt on reasonably objective terms with my mother's trajectory and, yes, there was sadness there too, but the impenetrable wall she surrounded herself with precluded the kind of empathetic response I was feeling now. Of course, over the years and through this most recent journey, I had been changing too and that accounted for part of the perspective.

Still, the whole thing made me ruminate about the various intensities of sadness. Earlier in the day, I had been researching some small lights for a photography project, and in all cases, the lights were defined by their position along a lighting scale rooted in temperature and that represented the variations from the warmth of a solitary candle to the expanse of a cloudless blue sky.

With this scale still in mind, and considering the players in my orbit, the response—the reading—I got from my mother was like magenta—no less sad in the overall evaluation but much cooler—while in Judy's case, the sadness burned brightly and was hot. More like the sun's spectrum.

I did not judge the extent to which, if at all, these reflections signified anything at all, nor did I feel any sort of guilt as I felt my heart responding to someone I barely knew. Beneath it all, I was aware that I was worried about Judy, even though it was fifty years down the road.

Then, it was beyond dusk and with a head full of conjecture (not to mention half a bottle of wine) and more questions than when I had started, it was time to get some dinner prepared. Patricia would be home soon and I was looking forward to that and some much needed rest.

Chapter Twenty-Three

Hailey's Comet

As I stood at the end of the driveway while Riley took inventory from the previous night, running erratically to and fro on the trail of an errant possum or skunk, the balance had shifted to a different set of considerations. Now, Watson, a new game was afoot.

I struggled with the way in which I could ask two important questions of my father. First, it was not clear to me—from memory or correspondence—whether the dissolution of my parents's marriage was driven by the affair with Judy or whether the reality was more linear—first Mom, then Judy, then Phyllis. Even as I considered what for many would be pedestrian facts, I was intrigued by how much I had been able to overlook during years past, and my limited appreciation of human behavior suggested perhaps an answer rooted in self-protection.

Nevertheless, it is still a source of frustration that I can remember nothing before the age of almost five, and for the period in question, I seem to have had no awareness of disharmony in the marriage or anxiety about the future. Without some intense transactional analysis, I could not imagine these issues getting clarified and the cost/benefit tradeoff was not worth it to me anyway.

It would be easy to pose the question of chronology to my father and I intended to do so in the near term. The more complicated consideration was where Judy had ended up, and it would be tough to raise this issue with him, since it would be loaded with significance beyond what I might present as basic curiosity. Asking would confirm what he might only imagine at this point: that in clearing out his house, I had discovered more than a cache of twenty-dollar bills stuffed in every corner. The whole issue of their house seemed now to be an abstraction for him, anyway, speaking of self-protective gymnastics. He never mentioned anything about it.

I was on my own in this quest, now, and resorted to the tools of the day. Ancestry websites were disappointing and Google just a bit less so, though it did provide me with her maiden name. I had been able to move rapidly on my mother's side back to the early 1800s in Northern Ireland and, after removing some obstacles on the Deane side, back to pre-Mayflower days in jolly olde England, so it was frustrating to come up empty handed as I tried to learn more about Judy Rubin.

It was the discovery of Judy's maiden name that was the breakthrough, ultimately. After trying various searches that included more than one word, I found connections that began to turn supposition to fact. With my newfound obsession, I returned to the hunt repeatedly, especially during the early morning hours before the workday began.

It was during one of early sessions that I found the first social security listing for Judy and this almost immediately enabled me to see that she had died in 1973. The bass line from the movie "Jaws" was playing (virtually) by then and at one point I jumped from my chair and interrupted Patricia as she prepared for a class that night by exclaiming, "Jesus! How weird would it be if...?"

Forward progress slowed repeatedly, but then, in another convoluted search attempt, I was presented with a set of high school yearbook pictures, including some from Hopedale, Massachusetts, and by working up from her birth in 1939, I was able to determine that she had been a cheerleader in Hopedale, at least during 1957.

Now that I was able to "triangulate" a bit with three pieces of data, I was able to work into the onion more. During one of the searches I did using "Hopedale," I was presented with a website page that offered a history of Hopedale's past, including stories and pictures and, in this case, an otherwise obscure reference to an Aerosmith concert that Judy had helped to make happen in some way. Just one sentence, deep within the rear caverns of the Internet. Apparently, she lived on the same street as one of the band members.

By looking at the source code for the web page, I was able to identify one of the authors and I took a leap and contacted him directly.

-----Original Message-----

From: Shaun Deane

Sent: Tuesday, September 20, 2016 11:39 AM

To: dantheman102@verizon.net

Subject: seeking information about Hopedale alumni

Hello Dan—

This is a complete shot in the dark but the power of the internet is not to be ignored. I am trying to determine what happened with a 1957 graduate of Hopedale HS. Her name was Judith Stevens and when married, last name Rubin. She passed away in 1973 and I am having a very difficult time finding out any information. I am writing a book about my family and there is a connection to my Dad, who was involved in a relationship with Judy in the late 60s and early 70s. He has dementia now so it is not possible to get any reliable information from him.

I don't know if you have any suggestions—perhaps a pointer to town records or something like that. I don't know where she was living at the time of her death, for example.

I am seeking this information because I suspect there is an unusual parallel to my mom's death and I'd like to confirm it so I can write my story with a little more confidence about any facts.

Sorry for the intrusion.

Shaun Deane

Brattleboro, Vermont

On Sep 20, 2016, at 4:36 PM, Dan Malloy <dang@verizon.net> wrote:

Hi Shaun,

I got her obit at the library and have attached it. To be more specific about her death than the paper was, the story at the time was that she had committed suicide in a motel, in Idaho. If you'd like to know more (though not about her death—that's all I know about that) let me know and I'll add a few more details.

Dan

After I had knee surgery in 2003, part of the rehabilitation therapy included jogging in the shallow end of a pool. I was always struck by the density of the water when I first got in and how much resistance there was (which was the point) and I felt like that as I read Dan's brief summary and then the actual obituary that he had included.

What had begun as a fantastic consideration that could not possibly have held up was now confirmed in the stark black and white article from the Hopedale newspaper. Someone, likely a librarian, had handwritten a date (2/17/73) at the top of the page.

Although I no longer drink caffeine, I felt as though I had downed a strong cappuccino, since my heart was racing. Oddly, and with a touch of guilt, I felt excitement. The truth shall set you free! But, in parallel, I also felt a profound sadness. This could not be. How could this possibly be true? Why Idaho? Seemingly ridiculous suppositions were racing, as if a desktop Rolodex was being twirled in front of me by an invisible hand. Just questions, no answers.

I used Google Maps to find Hailey, Idaho. That's just a stone's throw from Ketchum. Was she headed for Hemingway? Some sort of reunion? Back to Papa? This idea was crazy. What happened? Why?

Holy shit, holy shit.

Now, in addition to the cold and hard facts I had reviewed every single day since 1977, there was new information. I was gobsmacked. It felt as though someone had broadsided me with a two-by-four and it made me feel unsteady. I needed to verbalize what I now knew but did not yet understand or accept.

Dad. You prick.

The orbit of death surrounding him was more expansive than I had understood. I had been spending years trying to achieve "escape velocity" so that I could distance myself from the carnage that he attracted. My uninformed construct had been limited to those in my direct family, and now it was obvious that his impact was more pronounced than I ever could have imagined. The email I had printed out from Dan—my new, unknown friend—felt electric in my hands. The obituary included a professional photograph of Judy that I had in a box, directly under my desk, and that realization brought tears to my eyes.

All of it was yet another conduit to serve up the unexpected and the uninvited. Getting blind-sided—would it ever cease? At the end of it all, somehow, I had been spared.

Perhaps I should have felt empathy for him. Critiques of Judy from the letters I had found leapt back to the forefront of my consciousness. Intellectually, I knew that all failing relationships included such jabs. Emotionally, though, I was flummoxed and blaming. Forgiveness would come, I assumed, but it felt very far away in my small office, in late September. Synopsis: within four years, Dad's lover, his ex-wife, and his youngest son all opted for a permanent solution to a temporary problem.

I looked up from my computer screen and across to the open field across from our house. As far out as I could see, a red fox with a flared tail that skimmed the tall grass sauntered from left to right. Looking down, I was not surprised to see two large teardrops on my desk.

Later that week, there was one more email exchange with Dan, driven by my thanks for his efforts. His reply provided more detail but left me with a stronger hunger to know more, and to know it all, but that, it appeared, might continue to elude me since the principals were gone or incapable and the records were old.

On Sep 22, 2016, at 10:58 PM, <dantheman102@verizon.net> wrote:

Dear Shaun,

I don't know if you're familiar with Hopedale at all, but it's very small in area and population. Back when I was in high school, the town population was about 3000 and there were 27 in our graduating class. Judy's family was pretty well known in town. What I remember about her father was that he always introduced the band at the six band concerts at the town park every summer. At Draper, where most of the men in town worked then, he was listed in the street listing books for those years as a foreman. Judy had a brother and a sister, both older I think. What I noticed in the library scrap book I was looking through for her obituary was that her mother had died in 1973 also. I should have written down the date, but can find it if that would be of interest. I think it was early in the year, Jan or Feb, not long before Judy's death. Judy got pregnant when she was a high school senior. She married the father, her classmate, Roger Rubin. Roger was one of the star basketball players and Judy was a cheerleader. While I don't recall from the time, I presume she dropped out of school and he continued. In those days extra-curricular activities, other than the one that got them into the situation, were out for those involved, so Roger didn't play basketball that year. It was considered quite a loss to the team, but they went on to have an undefeated season. As you saw in the obituary, Judy finished school and was a top student at Clark. She taught at Nipmuc Regional High School. I taught elementary school in the same district. I don't know where Roger went to college, but he eventually became president of Home National Bank in Milford. Inquiring about this at the reunion today, I was told that he's now in a nursing home in Milford with an advanced case of Parkinson's. I don't know about her, but I don't think he would have been an easy guy to get along with. A year or two ago I was interviewing a guy in Mendon for his memories about when his father operated the Town Hall Spa, a restaurant in the Hopedale town hall. He told me that when Judy and Roger were first married they rented an apartment from someone in his family. They were known for having frequent and very loud arguments.

Dan

During the Labor Day holiday, I built a four-foot-long bookshelf from some beautifully figured cherry wood and, using a series of toggle bolts, affixed it to the wall just to the left of my desk. It is intended to be, literally, the top shelf for books I've read over the course of a lifetime and I like the idea that the shelf is finite in width and that only so many books can be accommodated. As I populated the shelf, I replaced tattered paperbacks with brand new hard covers.

At a certain point, new arrivals would have to slug it out with current residents in hopes of attaining exalted status. Some inclusions were no brainers, like *Moby-Dick*. My father had taught the book for years and it was perhaps his favorite novel.

I had taken, and loved, an entire course in Melville during my senior year in college. As I pulled the new copy that described the great white whale down from the right side of the long shelf, it felt to me as if my own tale had the scope of Melville's work.

A close friend summarized: "This is stunning. I mean, your dad could not have known this shit would happen. People do what they do. But it's an Ahab's story. The enormity of this. Wow. Judy sounds pretty remarkable and pretty damaged. Your dad no doubt loved her. Saw her as a wounded bird. She no doubt loved him."

Yes, no doubt.

And, I only am escaped alone to tell thee.

Chapter Twenty-Four

---•---

Goodbye

To Paul and Phyllis Deane

Dad and Phyllis, I know there's nothing I could say to make you feel any better about this. I know how you feel about me and I'm sure you know I feel that same way towards you. It's something that can't be said in words, so I won't try.

The only thing I feel bad about is that I could not be there to comfort you. Especially you, Dad. But you do have Phyllis, who is someone and something that is not comparable to anything in the world. I'm sure you know that.

And I'm counting on you, Phyllis to get him through this— like you have with everything else he or we have ever been through.

I guess I ought to thank you now, Phyllis, for everything you've always done. From helping in my mother's Death to those Sunday night dinners. That food was the only food I ever really enjoyed. Thanks again.

It seems like no one was ever thanking you for all the shit you did for us. I can't tell you how much it meant to me, except that if you hadn't been around these past years I probably would have done this long ago.

I guess I've been telling you how I feel, after all.

Dad you should know how I feel about you so I won't make this any worse. I guess I can't help it though. A thought just ran through my head about when Phyllis told me that if she had had a son, she would have wanted me to be it. If I had replied to that, I would have answered that had I the choice, Mother it would be not. Wife is what I'd want.

Feelings for you they weren't Dad (obviously). I guess I just wanted to let you know how fortunate a man I think you are and Phyllis how I felt about her. Brother, I hadn't planned on saying all this.

I would like to talk about money though. Seeing that Shaun has some money coming in now, and you'll be doing better without alimony payments, I was hoping to get some of it to my friends. I don't know it it's possible or not. I can't see why not. I've got five thousand dollars. I know some of it will be taken by Government or other people. But the people I'm talking about are:

Joe
Dale
Shawn
Liz

I could think of others but I haven't seen them in a while and don't know their money situations. These friends, I know, could use the cash. Do what you can, huh?

Don't look for any specific thing that set this off. It's been brewing for years, as you know.

After hearing you tell me you felt guilty about Mom's Death, I can imagine how you might feel now, but try and believe me when I say that you had nothing to do with it and that you could not have done anything about it for me. The same way I told you I did not feel guilty about Mom's Death—knowing that I could not do anything for her.

I can't think of anything else.

Give my love to Shaun.

Goodbye,

Christopher

Chapter Twenty-Five

Soufflé

Dear Chrissie
When I first met you
I gave you one of my treasures
Cheese soufflé
You loved it as much as I did
And so it came to be
That I made it many times
For you
And soon I was no longer
Making it for me
But making it for you
That made me very happy

Now you have put yourself
Under the ground
Sleeping and at peace
My treasure of cheese soufflé
Is lost to me
I no longer have power
To beat the eggs
And still less power
To place the soufflé on my tongue
And still less to swallow it

Cheese soufflé is gone from me
Forever
And much more.

July 13, 1978
Phyllis Horn Deane

Chapter Twenty-Six

2016

Too much wine (again) last night. Damn. It didn't take much those days to kick off the Nantucket sleigh ride. My gut was a swarm of butterflies and my hands did not have a home. My left arm bounced lightly on the armrest, which positioned my hand at nine o'clock on the steering wheel, but that felt awkward and created a crick in my neck so I shifted my hand to the top of the wheel at high noon—the power position of any confident pilot worth his salt—and then realized another two miles down the road that my knuckles were white from clutching the wheel so tightly.

We were headed north, to Conway, and had plans to knock off another 4000 footer in our attempt to climb all of the New Hampshire high peaks.

Breathe. Relax. I could never get that right. Too much oxygen left me feeling light-headed, so I'd revert to shorter breaths, making me feel like a Pomeranian on point within a minute or so.

Adjust the rear-view mirror, then flip it up as you do in the dark to minimize reflections—it meant less to monitor behind. Then back to position, trying to keep the sixteen-pound orb on top of my neck plumb, with my hand back in place, along my cheek line. While in this state, I would sometimes turn both side mirrors out as far as they would go in an attempt to reduce my awareness of what was approaching on all sides. "Look up! Texting and driving is not safe," proclaimed the solar powered

DOT sign on the side of the road.

My face was flushed. I stretched my neck to take stock (since the rearview was now in nighttime mode) and felt a bit like a prairie dog as I did so. The temporal arteries on my forehead were pronounced and I wondered whether this was a change.

The overriding concern was about loss of control. Maybe a mile down the road, I'd pull off into the breakdown lane, leave the car, and run across that field while tearing off my clothes.

I understood in a cognitive sense that my system, my being, could no longer tolerate the residual effect of what (for most) would be a small amount of ethanol from the previous evening. *You just do not metabolize stimulants well,* I thought, as I considered Mr. Boston, my eighth-grade science teacher, and thanked him for giving me that word. I once read that Edgar Allen Poe could get completely shitfaced on a tablespoon of liquor. Cheap date.

Yet at the end of any given day, I afforded myself a small reward for meritorious duty. Just to take the edge off, just to get the glow. It was becoming tedious, though, and the feature/benefit equation—which for many years had tipped in favor of "pleasure"—was, at best, even and oftentimes more work than it was worth.

I am a fast drinker. If Patricia is teaching a night course, I can have half a bottle of wine polished off before she has hit the bottom of the hill on her way to class. At that point, all that is left to me is, typically, another small glass since I know clearly that the anxiety train would be leaving Euston Station the next day if I exceeded my allotment.

Lurking behind me was always The Encourager—"But it ought to be okay. Just a little more."

Which is how I found myself on this Friday afternoon as we were heading north on the interstate to go hiking in the White Mountains of New Hampshire. It was sunny, the traffic was light, and Riley was asleep on the back seat. She, too, was pursuing her merit badge: to show that she had bagged all forty-eight peaks that surpassed four thousand feet. We had eight done and were shooting for numbers nine and ten this time out.

At the moment, though, I was trying to stay between the lane dividers. It felt as though I was driving on a Zoetrope.

The effect was that the road and the view were rolling toward me, creating some mild vertigo. I couldn't seem to find the sweet spot to observe. If I looked just in front of the car, I could see the grain in the asphalt in much more detail than I needed, and then, if I "got that big picture view" (and then I thanked Ed Weist, from Driver Education 101), it was entirely too much information and recalled the sensation of lying in bed when I was young and alternately feeling enormous in the bed and then microscopically tiny.

Epinephrine was being released in large amounts, and as I struggled with fight or flight, I was acutely aware of the responsibility I had beside and behind me, asleep on the back seat.

I jumped when, from the shotgun seat, Patricia said, "Rebecca just sent me a message. Olive slammed heads with another kid at school and got a concussion." Olive was seven.

"Poor kid," I grunted as I shifted in my seat and tugged at the neck of my T-shirt.

"Luckily Tim had a rental car today and was able to pick her up because Rebecca was at the farm. She's been puking so they can't give her anything until that stops."

"Huh," I offered in one of my most articulate moments as we took the exit for the east-west road that connected to the mountains about an hour away. Riley jumped up onto the rear armrest behind Patricia and pressed the window button so that the car was flooded with an unexpected breeze, and because no other windows were cracked, the interior of the car thumped like a Huey over Khe Sanh.

"Okay, Riley, need to roll 'em up," I said and pressed the window lock until the détente clicked under my left index finger.

Patricia asked, "How's the driving going?"

"Bit of a challenge."

"Well, you know I'll drive anytime."

"I know, thanks. I want to work through this, though."

She patted my right knee affectionately.

Acceptance. No judgment. It was still foreign to me and my heart expanded in response.

Once off the highway, things calmed down significantly. Hell, I could use all my mirrors now. It was 180 miles door-to-door and we'd make that in three hours, but I considered that, had I been alone, I would have left the interstate miles ago for side roads and limped along to the Top Notch Motel in the dark.

All of it felt dumb and like I ought to be able to manage better, but I withheld judgment as much as I could and reminded myself that in my new digs, my new life, I had created quiet and a place for things that had been buried for decades to get some air time. And these long dormant emotions were taking advantage whenever possible.

It was still light out, but there was a snap in the air and I was profoundly exhausted. When we had been hiking regularly during the previous season, we were well organized, all of our equipment consolidated in one corner of the basement so that the effort to get out the door required little thought.

Surprised by the crisp October chill in the air, I considered the muddled job I'd done of packing my own gear earlier that day. I had broken some cardinal rules in my clothing selections, and while I had multiple layers available, there were other gaps beyond my fashion choices. It was unusual for me to be less than organized for an outing like this and it reinforced the level of fatigue I'd been bearing and served as a warning as well.

While Riley investigated pet-friendly room 114, we could hear a cough from the next room. Ears up, she cocked her head to the right and forced out two muted barks in response.

"Shush—no need," I explained. New rules apply. Not quite satisfied, she finished off with a guttural rumble and moved off to inspect the bathroom.

The agenda was light: unpack the cooler and eat, watch the News Hour, and get ready for the early cast call at the bottom of Crawford Path.

The small refrigerator door had been open for a while as Patricia unloaded the cooler and I sat facing a blank wall to the right of the bureau that supported the flat screen television.

The butterflies were back, and while I was not having the physical challenges I had experienced in the car, I had moved on to considerations of basic mental health. *What is this tenuous hold we have on sanity,* I mused. What keeps me in the "now" versus some different plane where logic is absent and behavior is unpredictable? What if I snap? What would snap mean? Breathe. In, out. Don't worry Patricia. Pull it together. So tired, so very tired.

In the midst of this trance, I had not seen her approach. Kneeling in front of me, she ran her hands along the tops of my thighs. A sweet smile—communion. Sacrament accepted. As we embraced, tears sprinkled my lap and I sank into her safe harbor.

"I'm sorry," I said as I shook my head. "No one needs this."

"No, no!" she replied. "Everything is alright."

Later, lights extinguished, I lay on my back with my arms crossed, supporting my head, as the sounds in the room became familiar and the fraternity outside the room subsided as well. War weary but aware that sleep was still at bay, I considered my many gifts, including the capacity to forgive that I'd been offered and that I had taken decades to accept.

Smiling in the dark. Grateful. Counting examples up while reminding myself that there was no need to catalog. Steps approached along the covered concrete walkway that ran past the group of rooms in our block—a couple coming back from dinner. The low murmur of a man's voice, a pause, and then a lush giggle from just outside our door. I reached for Patricia's hand. And in reverie began to drift.

Hush now.

Chapter Twenty-Seven

Crawford Path

It was daybreak in the parking area just off the trailhead. We missed it the first time and ended up driving a few miles down the three-season road before making the call to turn around. Still, we had made good time over from the motel and now we stood outside the car assembling our gear for the hike up Mount Pierce and then over to Mount Eisenhower. Sipping tea from our Yeti containers, we spoke in monosyllables, mostly confirming that we had the necessities, since it had been a while—from before Patricia's hip surgery—that we'd performed these rituals.

"We lucked out," I said while craning my neck back. "No clouds today." And it was a gift, considering that it was the third week in October. A few degrees colder and a little less atmospheric pressure and we could have had a slippery day. The reassuring low tenor of the New Hampshire NPR broadcaster was describing that Hillary Clinton, up by three points in most polls, would be visiting the state again today.

Riley knew the drill. She sat calmly but could not help casting her imploring gaze at me every time it seemed that we were ready to go.

"Take it easy, buddy. Still need to get some stuff figured out," I explained.

A young college couple ambled by and the young lady said to her partner (and me, by association), "That dog looks like Cisco. Same shape."

"A low rider?" I offered, and they both smiled.

"Oh yeah, you gotta love those short legs—hard workers." This from the boyfriend.

"She's working on number ten today. Only thirty-eight to go," I said.

"Well good for you, shorty," said Riley's new friend as she reached down to deliver a quick belly rub.

Off they went, and Riley looked at me asking the obvious question—"Can I go, too?"

"Not yet. Almost time," I assured her.

After reconfirming that the keys to the car were safely stowed, we headed off across the lot and soon we were at the bottom of Crawford Path—"the oldest continuously used and maintained hiking trail in the Northeastern United States." It would be a little more than a mile before any map consultation would be necessary and we fell into an agreeable silence as we adjusted straps, shifted packs slightly, and considered whether our boots were laced comfortably enough.

The events of the previous evening were distant. I'd slept well, any toxins had been purged, and I found myself thinking of some lyrics to a song I had not heard since my stay in Seattle almost ten years before. My memory and the words were not in harmony but I could recall the first line: "When I awoke today, suddenly, nothing happened."

Suddenly. *The songwriter was rewarded right there,* I thought. Twists like that are gifts.

I could not recall what came next so I hummed to myself to try and get the timing right and then another line surfaced: "Down this beaten path, up this cobbled lane."

And I thought, *"Well, that's appropriate."*

Then I was counting steps with my right leg, just to see how much real estate a hundred paces would cover, though I didn't turn my head to look back as I met the target number. It ended up as an exercise in estimation.

"I'll bet it's eighty paces to the large maple at the bend up ahead," I thought and, taking the bet, I started to count.

As lead (and only) dog, Riley broke trail and added more steps by running off to the left or right, depending on the track that some deep woods resident had taken the previous night. The man was right—lots of extra steps on short legs.

Then I recalled the final line from the verse in the song with no name: "I'm walking in my old footsteps, once again."

I do hope this song is not with me all day, much as I like the words, and I smiled to myself.

I looked up the trail and watched Patricia's easy and systematic cadence up the path. It was clear to see the influence of dance. There was no struggle as she weaved easily in almost imperceptible switchbacks, around roots and the occasional jagged granite protrusion.

We had reached the junction of the trail where the Mizpah Cutoff continued straight ahead while the Crawford Path turned to the left. Once we took the turn, we settled in for what was promised to be a moderate ascent to the peak of Mt. Pierce.

It was still. The sun was up and painting amber doubloons on the leaves along the trail in front of us.

The pitch of the trail had increased slightly. It was helpful to dig the toes of my boots in a bit more aggressively with each step, for better purchase. Years of running long distances had provided many side benefits, so it was easy for me to fall into a familiar trance after each small break we took. There was something about the rhythmic motion that allowed me to focus on breathing and a slowing of the internal chatter that accompanies most waking moments and get me to a place of stillness much more quickly than sitting on a zafu cushion in my living room.

Two rollicking chipmunks tumbled across the trail in front of us. The first skittered into view on its back, cheeks bulging with at least two good-sized acorns. The impact dislodged one nut, which the pursuer quickly grabbed as it slowed for just a moment and then continued into the deeper foliage across the trail to the left. The scene from Bambi came to mind and Thumper was describing that the water was "stiff."

Then Chris was back. It had become standard fare over the years that when I started to slow down some, he'd appear. And it was really the abstraction or the idea of his reality that presented itself. It wasn't a rehashing, or an injection of regret or sadness, but more like punctuation or a road sign along a well-travelled path. A signal. Here we are at Exit 38 again—creating awareness of and space for the merge lane on the right. Then, incoming.

I have been stringing beads for forty years in an effort to create a narrative to explain the chaos I'd experienced for the twenty-some odd years beforehand. As I stepped over a very large and gnarled root that bisected the trail at a forty-five-degree angle, I knew that enlightenment was still at bay, but there was no denying that I had been gifted with some unexpected insights along the way and, especially, in recent years.

Stumbling along, trying to separate wheat from chaff, letting the rough side drag and the smooth side show. During the time when I was divorcing from Kate, the counselor I was seeing described that this rupture was driving a huge release of energy. It seemed to be a simple assessment of an obvious reality, but now I could see that it was profound.

It has been said that drug abusers or alcoholics "stall" emotionally at the time the addiction really takes hold, often in adolescence. It seemed clear to me that the family events I had experienced put the brakes on, too, and like a butcher's cleaver slamming through a thick rib eye steak, separated "then" from what followed. After the first volley came, a delayed but lengthy period of numbing self-flagellation followed. In a best effort at salvation, I grabbed for the raft that Kate and a structured suburban living might offer. I was trying to tidy up the mess.

With the tsunami in retreat and the promise of a rebirth in Vermont, I had become more still than at any previous time in my existence. It was unnerving much of the time but sorely needed. The decline of my father and stepmother has enabled me to witness some long-hidden truths. As I cleared out their home, my inheritance included a trove of source material that blew some of the fog off the landscape. I've been given a chance to return to that "stall point" and to make a return of sorts to the direction that might have been.

Riley was back and struggling with a stick that was too wide for the trail and that prevented forward progress. Most of the time when she hit a tree, she would turn her head sideways and figure out a way to make it through, but then she'd run into opposing bollards on the side of the trail that would stop her dead in her tracks. After she had tried to push through four times, I had to intercede.

I suppose that, like Riley, I'd been bashing into obstructions after Chris's death for an extended period with nothing more to show for it than a pretty consistent headache. I was beating myself up physically during the day by running longer and longer distances through every New England season, and at night I'd ingest whatever was available and close down the bars along Beacon Street in Brookline. It was not the best time to have owned a fast motorcycle.

When I met Kate at a barbecue in 1984, I was in the best shape of my life (physically) and I had a bit of swagger though I was lost inside. At that first meeting, she was interested, but I missed the signals completely. Months later on New Year's night, we met again at Nick's house and the ensuing twenty years were locked in quickly.

She had been through a rough patch, some bad luck, and all I could see was what to do. The situation satisfied my unconscious need to bury myself in purpose. It was not until years later that we'd actually get to know one another in an unfiltered way and a basic incompatibility became clear. Alignment of expectations and requirements were "off." I suppose that resolving that ratio is at the core of many relationships.

Now, as we passed through 3000 feet on the way to the summit of Mount Pierce, I considered a book I'd been given when things were falling apart with Kate that described some Toltec philosophy of The Four Truths. I did not retain much from the text except for a description of the belief systems that we receive as infants and that contribute to our worldview. Our parents shape these models. They provide messages about the world at large and our engagement with it.

During my divorce, it was liberating to understand that any model could be replaced—take what you need and leave the rest—and when I did, I was able to finally regroup and start to regain a true connection with the part of me that had been driven into the culvert so many years ago.

Like the product of a foundry, my personal crucible in Seattle burned off most of the impurities that had provided a history of stumbles and helped to prepare me for getting whole once again.

There, on a trail of a different type that ran along the West side of Lake Washington from Andrew's house out through the University of Washington campus, even my relationship with running changed. No longer a battle, my steps became wonderful meditations and private hours when I could shake off the intrusion of external and internal conversations, enabling me to see the landscape, and my place within it, in utter clarity. Then, as I made the turn to head home at points further and further away, I would look forward to the final stretch near home, under a canopy of dogwood trees that deposited a carpet of white petals and obscured all traces of the asphalt path, as I craned my neck for a glimpse of Big Ed.

The rake of the trail up Mount Pierce had increased. As I cut the pace back and shortened my steps, Judy was back and driving, frantically, toward Idaho. Why there? Why Idaho?

Slightly embarrassed, I had reached out to her son, who was now a resident of Idaho himself. What was the connection with that area? I did not really expect an answer and what little I had been able to find out about him—owner of a small electronics firm with a recent DUI—had done nothing to provide The Answer I sought. What did I really expect, anyway, except for more collateral damage?

After I met and then became engaged to Patricia, I sent her a dozen red roses for an occasion that I no longer can recall. A few months later, on one of my regular visits back to Vermont from Seattle, before it was time to turn in for the night, she brought me outside carrying a large silver salad bowl covered with a yellow dishtowel.

The gibbous moon was more than enough to light up the fields that stretched across to the site of the old mill that provided hydro power at the turn of the previous century. She slipped the towel off the bowl and I could see that it was filled with rose petals.

"Take one side of the bowl," she said softly. That sweet smile. Standing across from one another on the small hill next to the farmhouse and holding the bowl between us, our height difference was more pronounced, with her on the downside.

"This is for Chris," she explained and, with no instruction needed, we both snapped the bowl up over our heads just as a cold gust of wind ripped across the driveway and pulled the petals up and out in a crescendo above us. My eyes filled and it was hard to tell whether that was a response to the sudden gust of wind from the west or an emotional reaction to the beauty I had just witnessed and continued to see. A partner of substance. Speaking volumes with only a phrase.

As I trudged along the Crawford Path with Judy along for the ride, this interlude made perfect sense in some way.

Riley was impatiently banging her stick against the back of my right boot since her preferred position was between the two of us. As I stepped to the side to let her by, I considered the women in my father's life and their involvement in the dependency/savior cycle that I, as well, had succumbed to in my first marriage.

And then I was at the Hampton Beach Casino peering through a pair of stationary binocular cups into a five-foot-high box that was painted in red and blue clown colors, as the gentleman from the Monopoly game with the top hat used his cane to point at the words on the side of the box: "These Are Your Memories!" My right hand pushed a large silver wheel forward—a wheel polished smooth after generations of use and the humidity of the ocean boardwalk.

As I nudged the drum forward, the individual images merged imperceptibly into short movie clips that depended on my right hand for fluidity and grace, like a giant flip book. First up was Chris on a Dublin street corner in his tweed jacket, a copy of the *Irish Times* under his right arm as he squinted into the sun. Behind him on the entire sidewall of a small pub, the affirmation "Guinness is Goodness!" confirmed what I already knew to be true. His left hand held a pack of John Player Specials and he shook one out as an offering to me.

My mom—Betty, hopping off the chair lift at the top of the Blue Hills in Milton, and though the images were black and white, I could see her red hair as part of the autumnal tapestry behind and all around her, the leaves still clinging tightly before the October winds descended to rip them free. She hopped three times on her good leg as she smiled for the camera but then looked quickly away to the right. I used my hand to run this sequence backward and then forward a few times, eventually isolating each individual hop as her shorter left leg gamely played catch up.

Now Jim turning the corner onto Gilbert Street as I raised my hand again. No.

And then, inexplicably, a moment I had not thought of since it occurred. Idling behind a blue Plymouth Valiant at the intersection of Fuller and Chestnut Street, I was waiting to turn left, toward Waban, in my red and white Volkswagen bus, a few months after Chris had died. The car was full, and after three opportunities to initiate the turn had come and gone, I tapped my horn once. The occupants were just slightly younger than me and the passenger in the right rear seat turned his head to look at me as he flipped his greasy black hair back to get an unobstructed view. While pushing his friend away, laughing, he offered me his right middle finger as our eyes locked.

An enormous ocean roller of rage surged from my feet, through my torso, to my face—a flush. Without any hesitation, I flipped the shifter into neutral, pulled the emergency brake back toward me, and threw open the driver's door. As I ran toward the car, it finally pulled out into traffic, as the two droogs in the back seat laughed even harder and as I chased vainly onto Chestnut Street. Then, realizing it was futile, I leaned forward with my hands on my knees as a series of convulsive sobs racked my body. As I looked behind me, under my arm, I could see the door of my bus fully open, standing at attention, as I pivoted on my heel and tried to get control of my breath, my racing heart, and the slosh of adrenaline in my gut.

I looked up from the viewing drum as we turned a corner on the trail and some welcome unfiltered light warmed the path as we approached timberline. Riley dug at a large pinecone ahead of Patricia, and as I looked down at the roots in front of me, my hand coaxed the casino drum forward again.

Two quick vignettes next. In the first, I was in the rear seat of Judy's car as the rain pummeled her windshield and her hands white knuckled the wheel at the ten and two o'clock positions. "Radar Love" blared from the radio and up ahead the highway sign read "Elevation 2800 feet" and below that, on the same pole, "Entering Hailey." Next, dinner at my father's house with Phyllis to my left. Dinner was over, and the two taper candles in front of me flickered pleasantly as she placed her just lit Pall Mall in the ashtray in front of her and pushed along a small liqueur glass of Green Chartreuse to me and to my father. She pulled the starched white napkin off her lap as she exclaimed, "What I have to say, is rightee-ho!" and swung the napkin in circles over her head like M.L. Carr at a Boston Celtics playoff game.

According to the small map I had tucked inside my shirt pocket, we had another half mile to the next trail crossing and then a quick scramble to the cairn that would mark the summit of Mt. Pierce. Although it was not yet mid-morning, it was warm and I was anticipating and hoping for the breeze I suspected would greet us on top, out in the open. A quick adjustment of our pack straps and then we were off again, and I was back to the movies.

For the final act, inevitably, it was Dad. As I peered into the box intently, I tried, as always, to see something—to secure some insight into all that had happened in his life and the impact it all had on those around him. Since I had considered our relationship for a half century, it was easy to apply labels to events or behaviors. His "narcissistic personality disorder" precluded empathy and demanded the limelight. He suffered no competition. In his core, he was deeply insecure, yet boastful to keep from being exposed. The relationship choices he had made were consistent and, ultimately, tragic. What we needed, desperately, he withheld.

The challenge along the way has been to resolve his pattern of retreats: first from our "nuclear" family, then an exponential withdrawal into bitterness after Chris died and, after that, additional affronts.

He never visited anyplace I lived after 1985 and as a result has had no relationship with his two grandchildren. His explanation was straightforward—he did not like Kate—but the reality was that he sensed her distaste for him and that just didn't work in his construct that demanded center stage.

Throughout the decades, there has never been a glimmer of ownership, or remorse, or guilt, and because they are completely unresolved, it accounts for his most frequent assessment these days that "Shaun, I just don't know," as he shakes his head, slumped in the wheelchair that he propels with his feet at a centipede's pace.

Sometimes, when the subject of my son comes up, my father will retell a story of visiting us at my in-laws when Travis was young—no more than four years old. The Smiths lived close to the beach and by the water.

Walking along the shore, in the late morning fog, Travis asked, "Grandpa, what would you do if I threw a handful of sand at you?"

"Why, I'd knock you on your ass," came the reply and, according to Dad, Travis did, and then *he* did and they then walked hand in hand up to the house. This Hallmark card moment has always been presented as a victory by Dad, but for me, it only speaks to the great insecurity of a sixty-year-old man who had to stand tough against a sweet, young kid.

Ultimately, I see a man who has tried to apply the logic he found so reassuring in grammar, and his instruction of it, to life. His life. Of course, the conflict is that living, breathing beings do not behave logically and often need to be granted a pass and absolution. Now, I try to offer him as many of those things withheld as I can. A vain attempt to "kill 'em with kindness," perhaps, but as I have evolved incrementally, the gift I have taken away has been the opportunity to unencumber myself from the anger and bitterness that suffocate him daily.

The blind squirrel sometimes finds an acorn.

And now it was time to step away from the casino game and to rejoin the clamber up the final patch of scree as we approached the summit of Mount Pierce.

As we turned the corner for the final push to the cairn, the entire valley of Crawford Notch State Park unfurled itself beneath, and behind us. Mount Washington, looking benevolent out in the distance, had always been a touchstone in Patricia's family. She was wearing her father Roger's large red framed ski glasses in tribute, and she mouthed the word "Wow!' over her shoulder at me as we both recognized our incredible fortune on this day and in everything else.

And then, standing side by side at the summit with my arm around Patricia's waist, we were surrounded by a cacophony of sounds but no noise.

I looked at this gift in my arms and out across the ridge to Mount Eisenhower in the brilliant October sunshine that warmed my neck from behind, as Riley slurped from the water bowl I had placed exactly on top of the geological marker that indicated the true summit.

And, I realized that one of my greatest accomplishments had been to purge myself of the anger that had been presented as a model of acceptable behavior in the belief system that I had been handed years ago and that I had now rejected. When I did, love rushed in. The circle had been broken. I looked at Patricia again and down at Riley and it was good.

Yes.